Sniff Squad: Dog Training for Kids Who Love Mysteries

Family Fun Activities, Detective Games, and Adventures for Kids Teaching Dogs Scent Skills

Agent Max

SNIFF SQUAD

Dog Training for Kids Who Love Mysteries

Agent ✼ Max

Family Fun Activities, Detective Games, and Adventures for Kids Teaching Dogs Scent Skills

Copyright © 2025 by Agent Max

All rights reserved. No part of this publication may be reproduced, stored in a retrieval system, or transmitted in any form or by any means -electronic, mechanical, photocopying, recording, scanning, or otherwise – without the prior written permission of the copyright owner, except in the case of brief quotations used in critical reviews or scholarly articles.

This book is a work of original authorship and is protected under the copyright laws of Australia and other countries, including international treaties such as the **Berne Convention** and the **Universal Copyright Convention**. Unauthorized reproduction, distribution, or adaptation of this work, in whole or in part, is strictly prohibited and may result in civil and criminal penalties.

This publication may not be used for commercial purposes, educational reproduction, or derivative works without express written consent from the copyright holder.

First Edition, 2025

Published by Imperium Ink

ISBN: 978-1-7644347-0-6

To every young recruit who follows their nose, solves mysteries, and believes in the power of teamwork – this book is for you!

To the legendary Super Sniffers who inspired it all: Cassius, Dexter, Maximus and Lucio – your noses led the way.

And to Dion – my partner, Editor, and the sharpest red pen in the Southern Hemisphere. Without you, this book wouldn't be half as polished, make nearly as much sense, or be as grammatically correct.
As usual, you are always right.
Thank you.

Contents

Introduction	1
1. Sniff Squad Academy	3
2. The Mind Behind the Mission	17
3. Super Sniffer Science	29
4. Ghost Scent Trails	41
5. Smell & Tell	51
6. Lead Like a Legend	63
7. The Great Indoor Drift	75
8. Grid Sweep Ops	87
9. It's All Elementary	97
10. Operation Crumb Bandit	109
Conclusion	123
About the Author	125
Welcome to HQ	127

Introduction

WELCOME, RECRUIT!

I'm Agent Max – Chief Sniff Squad Commander, certified Super Sniffer, and your guide through this top-secret training manual. If you've ever watched your dog's nose twitch with curiosity or wondered what invisible trails they're following, you're in the right place! You and your dog are about to unlock a world of scent, science and sleuthing that most humans never get to see.

Every dog, whether they're a bouncy Beagle or a sleepy Shepherd, comes equipped with a superpower: their nose. It's not just good. It's legendary! Dogs can detect scent particles in the air, on the ground, and even days after they've been left behind. With the right training, your dog's nose can help solve mysteries, track missing people, and decode the world in ways no machine ever could.

That's where you come in. As a Sniff Squad Recruit, you'll learn how to work as a team with your dog to become a real-life detection duo. This book is your official training manual. Inside, you'll find missions, scientific facts about how scent works, and mystery challenges that will stretch your skills and sharpen your instincts.

We'll start with simple searches and build up to adventures that incorporate the methods and training of real K9 search dogs. You'll learn how to read your dog's sniff signals, understand how scent travels, and use terrain and clues to guide your search. You'll also earn badges along the way – real achievements that mark your progress from rookie recruit to certified Sniff Squad Detective.

Whether your dog is a playful pup or a wise old veteran, these missions will strengthen your bond, boost their confidence, and give you both a new way to explore the world together.

So, are you ready to begin your training? Grab your gear, flip to your first mission, and prepare to sniff, search, and solve like never before. The world is full of mysteries, and your dog already has the nose to find them!

See you in the field!

Agent Max

Chief Sniff Squad Commander

P.S. Before you begin training, there's something you should know. Dr. Whiff, Chief Intelligence Agent at Sniff Squad HQ, has been tracking a trail of snack sabotage. Someone – or something – has been scattering crumbs across HQ zones, disrupting scent trails and leaving behind baffling clues. No pawprints. No sightings. Just crumbs… and chaos. We call this elusive figure *The Crumb Bandit*. Their identity remains a mystery, but their mischief is unmistakable. That's why we're calling on our newest recruits. You and your canine partner have the nose, instincts, and courage to help Dr. Whiff crack the case. As your training unfolds, you'll be called on to assist in solving top-secret scent mysteries, and help uncover the truth behind the Bandit's crumb-spreading spree. Stay sharp. Trust the trail. Every sniff will bring us closer to unmasking the Crumb Bandit!

Chapter One

Sniff Squad Academy
Day One Orientation!

Congratulations, Recruit! Today marks the beginning of your official journey as a **Sniff Squad trainee**. You and your four-legged partner are about to unlock one of the most powerful and often overlooked superpowers in the animal kingdom: the canine nose. Whether your teammate is a tiny Terrier or a towering Great Dane, every dog comes equipped with a **scent detection** system so advanced, it rivals the most sophisticated scientific instruments. Their nose isn't just for sniffing snacks or greeting other dogs – it's a high-resolution radar that can track movement, detect emotion, and even locate missing people. And today, you'll begin learning how to harness that incredible ability.

How This Book Works: Your Sniff Squad Training Manual

Before we dive into the world of canine communication, scent sleuthing, and tail-wagging teamwork, let's take a moment to sniff out what's ahead. This isn't just a book, it's your official Sniff Squad training manual. And like any good detective academy, we've got a plan.

Each chapter begins with a **Mission** – your top-secret briefing from Dr. Whiff at Sniff Squad HQ. Your mission card tells you exactly what your challenge is for the chapter. It might be about understanding how your dog thinks, teaching them a new skill, or solving a mystery together. So don't skip it! Reading the mission card first helps you know what to look for, what to practice, and what kind of detective work you'll be doing with your dog.

Most missions involve **both you and your dog** learning something new side by side. You'll be training, observing, experimenting, and recording your findings, just like a real scent detective. Your ultimate goal? To become a certified **Sniff Squad Detective**, one mission at a time.

But it's not all action and adventure. Every chapter also includes **important knowledge** to help you understand your dog's incredible abilities. You'll learn about the science of sniffing, how dogs learn, how to train with kindness and clarity, and how to build a bond that makes every mission more fun and effective.

No Sniff Squad chapter is complete without a **Super Sniffer Mystery**, and this is where the real detective work begins. Each Mystery Alert comes directly from Dr. Whiff at Sniff Squad HQ. These top-secret transmissions are designed to help you level up your skills, sharpen your instincts, and put everything you've learned into action. But they're not just training exercises, they're part of a bigger mission. Every Super Sniffer Mystery brings you one step closer to uncovering the truth behind the Crumb Bandit. As you work through each mystery, you'll gather clues, test ideas, decode your dog's signals, and unlock new ways to think like a real scent detective. The more mysteries you solve, the closer you get to cracking the case.

After each mystery is solved, you'll complete a short **Readiness Checklist** to make sure you've mastered the key ideas. Then – drumroll, please – you'll unlock your **Sniff Squad** badge! There's one badge for every mission. Earn them all to prove you've got what it takes to be a top-tier scent detective.

Oh, and keep your eyes peeled for **Super Sniffer Science Alerts** sprinkled throughout the book. These bite-sized fact bombs reveal amazing things about your dog's nose, brain, and behavior. They're quick, fun, and guaranteed to make you say, "Whoa, I didn't know that!"

So grab your field journal, leash up your canine sidekick, and get ready to train, sniff, and solve your way through the pages ahead. The Crumb Bandit is out there, and every chapter brings us one step closer to uncovering his next move... Let your first mission begin!

Mission #1: Complete Your Orientation

Mission Incoming!

Recruit, your first official assignment has just arrived, and it's urgent. **Dr. Whiff, Chief Intelligence Agent** at Sniff Squad HQ, has issued your first alert: more crumb mayhem has been discovered in the HQ grounds. Scent trails are scrambled. Clues are disappearing. The Crumb Bandit has struck again.

Before you can join the ranks and help crack the case, you must complete your Sniff Squad orientation. This chapter is your launchpad, the foundation for every mission to come.

You'll get a quick introduction to your dog's incredible sniffing abilities, just enough to spark curiosity and show why your canine partner is the ultimate scent detective. Then it's time to gear up. You'll learn how to assemble your **Sniff Squad toolkit**: scent containers, treat pouch, leash, reward systems, and your trusty field journal. Every item has a purpose, and you'll discover how to use each one to set your dog up for sniff-tastic success.

Next, you'll master the golden rule: **Safety First, Sniff Second**. You'll learn how to keep every search safe, focused, and fun. From leash control and dog-friendly zones to environmental awareness and respectful handling, this section ensures you and your canine partner are mission-ready.

This isn't just orientation, it's your first step toward becoming a certified scent detective. Complete every section, earn your Sniff Squad Recruit badge, and prepare to join Dr. Whiff's recruit team. The trail is fresh, the clues are fading, and the Crumb Bandit won't wait.

Let's get sniffing!

Introducing Your Dog's Super Sniffer

Have you ever wondered why your dog's nose is always cold and wet? Or why they insist on sniffing every tree, lamppost, and blade of grass on your daily walks? That curious nose isn't just for show, it's a built-in superpower, ready to be unleashed.

In fact, your dog's nose is more than powerful – it's a scent-detecting super lab! While humans have about 6 million **scent receptors** in their nose, your dog has over 100 million. And some top-tier sniffers, like Bloodhounds, boast an astonishing 300 million scent receptors!

That's why your canine companion can detect smells thousands of times better than you can. It's like being able to smell a crumb of cheese in an entire football stadium. That's not magic, it's science. And it's exactly why your canine is the perfect partner for cracking clues and chasing down trails.

As you begin your Sniff Squad training, remember, you're teaming up with one of nature's most advanced scent detection systems. Your dog already has all the tools they need to become an extraordinary scent detective. What they need now is your guidance to help them focus their super sniffer with purpose and precision.

We'll dive deeper into the science of your dog's nose in a later chapter. But before you can start solving mysteries, you'll need to gather the essential gear for your scent detection missions. And don't forget, the most important tool of all is already built in: your dog's incredible nose!

Gear up for Greatness: Your Scent Detection Kit

It's time to gear up for your first detection assignment! Just like any good detective, you'll need the right tools for the job. Let's explore the essential equipment that will help you and your canine partner become successful scent detectives.

First, let's talk about your **training pouch** - this will be your recruit utility belt! You'll want a pouch that clips around your waist or has a shoulder strap, making it easy to access treats quickly when your dog makes a successful find. Remember, timing is super important when rewarding your dog, so having treats readily available is crucial for effective training. Having the right treats in your training pouch will make a significant difference in your success - and keeping them separated in plastic bags will help retain their individual smells.

For **treats**, choose something healthy your dog absolutely loves but only gets during training sessions. This makes the rewards extra special! Small, soft treats work best because your dog can eat them quickly and get right back to searching.

Next, you'll need some **basic search equipment** – see our list below. When you're first starting out, you don't need it to be fancy. Many successful Sniff Squad teams begin with simple cardboard boxes or disposable plastic cups from around the house. These make perfect hiding spots for your early training sessions! As you advance, you can create your own scent detection kit and include interesting scents from basic items you might find in the pantry – soap, vinegar, sauces, vanilla essence or food flavourings can be dabbed onto cotton balls or swabs and stored separately in plastic ziplock bags.

Keeping your equipment clean is super important! Just like a real Detective needs to keep their tools in good condition, you'll want to store all your scent training items in separate, airtight containers or plastic ziplock bags. Clean any containers regularly with unscented soap, replace cotton swabs and other disposable items regularly, and keep a special bag or box just for your detection equipment.

As you progress through your Sniff Squad training, keeping a **field journal** can be a fun and valuable way to track your journey. This can be a simple notebook where you jot down the types of searches you practiced, which hiding spots were most effective, and how your dog signalled that they'd found the scent. Recording your **successes and challenges** helps you spot patterns, celebrate progress, and fine-tune your teamwork with your canine partner. Over time, your field journal will become a personal case file – filled with clues, discoveries, and the story of how you and your dog became scent detectives!

Here's a cool fact: professional detection dogs often work with specialized equipment, but they all started just like you - with simple training tools and lots of patience! Remember, you don't need expensive gear to start your scent detection adventure. Many of the best detection dogs started their training with simple household items! The most important things are consistency, patience, and having fun with your four-legged partner.

Safety First, Sniff Second

Before you head out on a scent mission, there's one thing every Sniff Squad Recruit must learn: **safety comes first**, for both you and your canine. Whether you're searching in your backyard, a bush trail, or a busy park, it's super important to look around for anything dangerous. That means checking for broken glass, prickly or poisonous plants, or nearby roads. Outside the house, make sure you have a parent or other grown up supervising. A safe space helps your dog sniff with confidence and helps you stay focused too!

SUPER SNIFFER SAFETY

- ✓ Always supervise your dog during training
- ✓ Use a leash on your dog when training in public spaces or anywhere they could escape
- ✓ Keep scented items out of reach until needed
- ✓ Use only safe, dog-friendly materials and treats (i.e. no chocolate!)
- ✓ Be mindful of weather conditions (is it too hot or cold) and avoid training in extreme weather
- ✓ Keep training sessions shorter on warm days to prevent your dog from getting tired or dehydrated
- ✓ Make sure your dog has access to fresh water during training
- ✓ Ask an adult to help prepare training equipment and for supervision when training outside the home

Next up is **leash safety**. Sometimes you'll use a long leash so your dog can explore more freely. Other times, you'll keep them close to guide them. Hold the leash so your dog feels calm and supported. And here's a tip: always stand beside or behind your dog, not in front, so you don't block their "scent cone" (that's the invisible area where smells float in!).

Sniff Squad Recruits always check the **weather** before heading out. If it's super hot, dogs can get tired, overheat quickly, or burn their paws from walking on hot pavement – so bring water, take breaks, and train in the shade or on grass. On rainy days, be careful of slippery paths. Cold weather can be fun too, but make sure your dog stays warm and dry. No matter the forecast, smart sniffers dress for the day, pack the right gear, and know when it's time to head home. A safe sniffer is a smart sniffer!

Even the best sniffers need a plan for surprises. Learn what to do if your dog gets tired, overheated, or needs a break. You'll also follow the Sniff Squad code: leave no trace, be kind to nature, and keep your search area clean. When you follow these safety rules, you're not just helping your dog, you're showing the world you're a smart, respectful scent detective!

We'll soon learn about how dogs learn new skills. But first, make sure you have your basic gear and memorize the safety protocols ready for your first assignment. Your adventure as a Sniff Squad Recruit is about to begin!

Badge Readiness Checklist

Before you unlock your first badge, make sure you've completed all the steps below. Tick each box once you've mastered the skill, cracked the clue, or completed the challenge. Are you ready to earn your badge?

I'm ready!

- ☐ I packed my training pouch with high value (i.e. extra yummy) treats.
- ☐ I collected at least 3 basic scent training tools (like boxes, containers, or cotton swabs).
- ☐ I chose a few household scents (e.g. vanilla, vinegar, or soap), to scent my cotton swabs, which I then stored in sealed bags for future training sessions.
- ☐ I have memorized the safety rules.
- ☐ I have checked my training area for safety hazards like sharp objects or toxic plants.
- ☐ I have set up a dedicated field journal ready for recording my dog's search patterns and successes.
- ☐ I am ready for my first mission!

Badge Unlocked: Sniff Squad Recruit!

Well done, Recruit! You've officially earned your **Sniff Squad Recruit** badge. That means you're now ready to sniff out clues, crack tricky cases, and become a teammate to your scent-savvy dog.

Mission Debrief: Orientation Complete!

Boom! You did it, Recruit! You've just wrapped up your first official day at Sniff Squad Academy – and the adventure is only beginning. Today, you and your canine partner unlocked the secrets of your dog's **amazing nose**, geared up with your first **detection tools**, and laid the foundation for a bond that's about to become legendary.

You've stepped into a world where scent tells stories, socks become clues, and every sniff could crack a case. You're not just training a dog – you're building a detection duo with instincts, strategy, and unstoppable teamwork. And guess what? You're already showing signs of greatness.

From here on, the missions get wilder, the mysteries get twistier, and your dog's nose gets sharper. You'll be tracking trails, decoding distractions, and solving scent puzzles that would stump even seasoned pros. Each chapter brings new challenges, new badges, and new ways to level up your skills.

In fact, just as you were wrapping up this first mission, a high-priority alert came in from Dr. Whiff at Sniff Squad HQ: there's been a confirmed sighting of the Crumb Bandit inside the Sniff Squad zone! Witnesses caught only a fleeting glimpse, but it was unmistakable. A masked figure in a purple cape and hat, vanishing into the shadows before anyone could intercept. The chase is officially on!

Keep your eyes peeled, Recruit… because in the next chapter, we're cracking open the secret vault of your dog's mind. You'll uncover what drives their sniffing superpowers, what ignites their decisions on the trail, and how to build a connection so strong, it feels like you're reading each other's thoughts.

Sniff Squad is just getting started. See you at the next training session!

Chapter Two

The Mind Behind the Mission
Unlocking Your Dog's Inner Detective

Welcome back, Recruit. Congratulations on completing your Orientation – well done! Now, it's time to get to work! With your gear packed and your field journal in hand, you're about to uncover one of the most powerful tools in the Sniff Squad arsenal: your **dog's mind**. This chapter takes you into the depths of **canine learning**. Understanding your dog's brain is the foundation of every mission ahead. Let's dive into the science and learn about what makes your canine tick.

Mission #2: Decode Your Dog's Mind

Recruit, your second mission has landed, and it's mind blowing!

This mission is all about unlocking the way your dog's mind works: how they **learn**, what drives their decisions, and how your energy and reward practices shape their success. You'll dive into the science of **association learning**, where actions and rewards form powerful patterns in your dog's brain. You'll learn to spot those patterns, reinforce them with precision, and build a training style that's both effective and fun.

At the heart of this mission is **motivation**: discovering whether your dog is powered by treats, toys, or praise. But motivation is only half the story. You'll also explore how dogs read your body language, respond to your enthusiasm, and thrive when training feels like a game.

And don't forget – Dr. Whiff is still on high alert. After last night's confirmed sighting of the Crumb Bandit near HQ, the faster you master your dog's learning style, the sooner you'll be ready to help crack the case.

Decoding the Canine Mind: How Does Your Dog Learn New Skills?

Dogs are natural learners, and their brains are wired for something scientists call **association learning**. This means they build connections between actions and outcomes. "When I sit, I get a treat." "When I follow that smell, I find something exciting!" These cause-and-effect discoveries help your dog create a mental map of what's worth doing again. The more positive the outcomes they experience, the stronger those connections become.

Think of your dog's brain like a pattern-hunting supercomputer. Every-time an action is followed by something good – whether it's a snack, a squeaky toy, or your enthusiastic cheer, their brain logs it as a win. These wins don't just shape behavior; they build confidence, motivation, and a sense of purpose. Over time, your dog learns which actions lead to rewards and which ones don't, forming the foundation of all future training.

But here's the twist: dogs aren't just learning from the environment, they're learning from *you*. They're expert **social learners**, constantly tuning in to your body language, tone of voice, and emotional energy. If you're excited, they're excited. Your reactions become part of the reward system, which means your enthusiasm isn't just helpful, it's essential. When you celebrate their success, you're reinforcing the behavior and deepening your bond. Understanding this learning process is the key to becoming a great trainer. It's not just about giving commands, it's about creating clear, consistent, and joyful experiences that help your dog thrive.

Training That Clicks: Teach Like a Pro

Now that you know how your dog learns, it's time to put that insight into action. Every Sniff Squad mission relies on association learning, so your job is to create clear, consistent, and rewarding experiences that help your dog connect the dots. Ready to train like a pro? Here are your key tips:

- ❖ Keep sessions short and upbeat – 5 to 15 minutes is ideal.
- ❖ Use positive rewards: treats, toys, or enthusiastic praise.
- ❖ Begin in quiet spaces, then slowly add distractions.
- ❖ Teach in small steps then build complexity.
- ❖ Celebrate every win, even the tiny ones.
- ❖ Reward right away – immediate rewards help them learn faster through association.
- ❖ Stick to the same cues and signals each time.
- ❖ Be patient—every dog learns at their own pace, and every step forward counts.

The Motivation Matrix: What Drives Your Dog?

Every great detective needs a reason to chase the case, and your dog is no different. To train effectively, you'll need to uncover what drives your canine: **treats, toys, or praise**. Breed history offers powerful clues, since many dogs were developed for specific jobs that shaped their natural motivators. Once you crack that code, training becomes smoother, faster, and way more fun.

Food and Praise Fanatics – Many dogs are natural scavengers, bred to track, retrieve, or search, making food a top reward. Labradors, Golden Retrievers, and Beagles will work hard for a tasty bite, while Cocker Spaniels respond well to both snacks and praise. Bloodhounds, famous for their scent-tracking skills, often need high-value treats to stay focused. These dogs thrive on quick, consistent rewards and are usually easy to train when snacks are involved. If your dog gets excited at the sight of a treat pouch, this might be their driving force.

Toy-Driven Dynamos – Dogs bred for herding, chasing, or high-energy tasks often prefer toys over food. Border Collies and Australian Shepherds love movement and interactive play, while Jack Russell Terriers bring relentless energy to chase-based games. Miniature Schnauzers often favor toys, and Belgian Malinois channel their intense working drive through tug games and fast-paced challenges. These breeds shine when training feels like a game. If your dog gets the *zoomies* at the sight of a ball, you've got a toy-driven dynamo.

Praise & Affection Seekers – Some dogs were bred for loyalty, protection, or companionship, and they thrive on human connection. German Shepherds respond best to trusted praise, Great Pyrenees value calm encouragement, and companion breeds like Cavalier King Charles Spaniels, Shih Tzus, and Newfoundlands train best when rewarded with attention and affection. For these dogs, your voice, touch, and enthusiasm are everything. If your dog leans in for cuddles after a job well done, this is likely their motivator.

But remember, every dog is unique, so it's up to you to test, observe, and confirm which motivator sparks their best performance. Only then, will you know how your dog truly likes to be rewarded.

Super Sniffer Mysteries Activated!

Recruit, the chase is on! HQ just dropped your first **Mystery Alert** – and it's your moment to dive into action, unleash your dog's sniffing superpowers, and earn your next badge.

These aren't just fun missions – they're part of a top-secret plan to stop the Crumb Bandit's snack-fueled sabotage. Every mystery is a chance to crack a case, level up your skills, and prove you're ready for the next challenge.

Dr. Whiff only sends alerts when he knows you're ready - so gear up, get ready to test your training, follow the instructions below, and learn the skills you'll need to outsmart the Bandit. Your first mystery is just over the page!

For Every Super Sniffer Mystery:

- ☐ Read the Incoming Mystery Alert from HQ
- ☐ Follow your Sniff Squad Orders to understand your mystery challenge
- ☐ Check off your Mission Checklist and prep your training space
- ☐ Follow the Sniff Instructions for step-by-step guidance on what you need to do
- ☐ Work through all three Mystery Levels in order
- ☐ Observe your dog and log your outcomes in your Field Journal
- ☐ Complete the challenge to earn your badge
- ☐ If you're a younger recruit, review the Parent Tips with a grown up

Super Sniffer Mystery
The Great Decoy Drop

Incoming Mystery Alert!:

A covert transmission has been intercepted: the Crumb Bandit is planning to deploy a decoy that matches your dog's biggest temptation — all to lure them off the scent trail. Is it a crunchy snack, a bouncing toy, or a burst of praise? To stay one step ahead, you must uncover what motivates your dog before the Crumb Bandit strikes. The clock is ticking and time is of the essence!

Sniff Squad Orders:

Your objective is to uncover what motivates your dog the most. Is it snacks, squeaks, or snuggles? Run the tests, log the results, and report back with your findings.

Mission Kit Checklist:

- ❑ Treats (extra tasty and not so tasty options)
- ❑ Toys (tug, squeaky, or fetch-style)
- ❑ Coloured, plastic cups to hide treats in
- ❑ Field journal or notebook for recording sniff strategy and mission outcomes
- ❑ Your canine detective, alert and ready
- ❑ A quiet training zone with space to play

Parent Tips for Younger Recruits:

Let kids lead the way and help with setup and timing. Use drawings to record results. Celebrate every win and be patient with your dog!

Sniff Instructions:

1. Choose a quiet space with minimal distractions—somewhere your dog can focus without too much noise, movement, or excitement.
2. Test one motivator at a time (treats, toys or praise) using the Mystery Levels below. This helps you spot clear patterns without mixing signals.
3. Watch your dog's reactions closely—look for tail wags, zoomies, eager eyes, or signs of boredom.
4. Use words or drawings to record your results and observations in your field journal.
5. Compare results to see which motivator sparked the most excitement. Write down the order of what worked, with 1 being the most motivating and 3 being the least motivating.
6. Celebrate your findings—you've cracked the first Sniff Squad mystery! You now know what motivates your dog the most – whether it be treats, toys or praise.

Level 1

Treat Test

- Offer a tasty treat after a simple cue like "sit" or "shake"
- Hide a treat under a cup or towel—does your dog sniff it out?
- Try a less tasty treat—notice any change in effort or excitement?

Level 2

Toy Test

- Offer a favorite toy after your cue - watch for tail wags or zoomies.
- Hide the toy—does your dog search or give up quickly?
- Play tug or fetch with the toy - see how long they stay engaged.

Level 3

Praise Test

- Offer praise, pats and tummy rubs after your dog actions a cue.
- Repeat the cue, but offer only verbal praise after completion.
- Repeat the cue but this time only offer gentle affection - see if they stay close or wander off.

Badge Readiness Checklist

Mystery solved, Recruit! You've cracked it – figuring out what truly motivates your dog. That's a huge win in the world of canine communication!

Before you unlock your **Mind Mapper** badge, make sure you've completed these final steps. Each one sharpens your skills and brings you closer to becoming a Sniff Squad Detective – you must complete all of them to earn your badge. Tick them off as you go!

I'm ready!

- ❏ I understand how dogs use association learning to connect actions with rewards.
- ❏ I practiced reading my dog's body language, including tail wags, focus, and energy.
- ❏ I tested all three motivators – treats, toys, and praise – and worked out which one motivates my dog the most, the second most & the least.
- ❏ I used consistent cues and signals (e.g. "sit") during training to help my dog learn faster.
- ❏ I kept my training sessions short and positive to boost my dog's confidence.
- ❏ I recorded my dog's reactions and discoveries in my field journal.
- ❏ I stayed alert for signs of the Crumb Bandit near the training zone!

Badge Unlocked: Mind Mapper!

Boom! Badge Unlocked! Congratulations, Recruit, you've officially earned your **Mind Mapper** badge! You cracked the code behind your dog's learning style and uncovered what truly motivates them. With this insight about your dog, every mission ahead will be sharper, faster, and way more fun.

Mission Debrief: Decoding Your Dog's Mind Complete!

Bravo, Recruit! You've just cracked one of the most vital codes in your Sniff Squad journey – decoding your dog's **mind and motivation**. By testing treats, toys, and praise, you've uncovered how your canine partner learns, communicates, and thrives. That's elite-level insight, and it's the kind of intel that separates rookies from real detectives.

Your field journal should be packed with clues, reactions, and "aha!" moments. These discoveries will fuel every mission ahead, from scent games to search drills; and help you train smarter, reward better, and build an unstoppable bond with your dog.

But stay alert... the Crumb Bandit's evil plans may have been foiled this time, but we've received intelligence that he was spotted near the training grounds. He's watching. He's scheming. And he's testing our readiness.

Every mystery you solve brings us closer to catching him, and unmasking the mind behind the crumbs.

Next up: your first official scent detection mission. You'll dive into the science of your dog's nose, prep your search zone, and learn how to sniff out hidden targets like a true undercover agent.

Stay sharp, stay curious, and keep your nose to the ground, this chase is just heating up!

Chapter Three

Super Sniffer Science
Unleashing Your Dog's Super-Sniffer Powers

HEADS UP, SNIFF SQUAD Recruit – your training just levelled up! You've figured out what makes your dog tick, from tasty treats to tail-wagging praise. Now it's time to tap into their greatest gift: **their sniffer**. This chapter kicks off your next mission, where you'll uncover the secrets of scent and learn how your dog's nose turns invisible smells into real clues. You'll explore the **science behind sniffing**, discover how your dog smells, and start building the skills to train like a top-tier scent detective. Ready to unlock your dog's super sniffer? Let the mission begin!

Mission #3: Operation Follow Your Nose

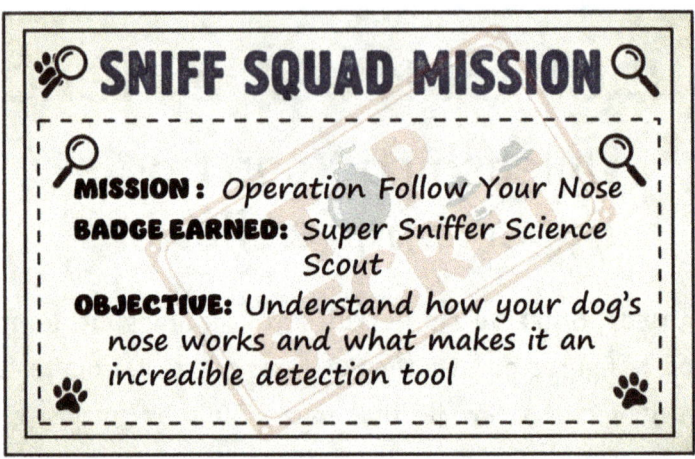

Recruit, your next mission from Sniff Squad HQ has just landed, and it's a big one. Dr. Whiff has confirmed a suspicious sighting near the HQ kitchen. The Crumb Bandit was seen snooping around, and it's only a matter of time before a new Mystery Alert drops. That's why this chapter is critical: you need to be ready.

This mission kicks off your deep dive into the world of **scent science** – where invisible trails become clues, and your dog's nose becomes the ultimate detective tool. You'll uncover how your dog's sniffer works like a stereo system, using both nostrils to detect direction and distance. Their brain doesn't just smell, it builds a scent map, decoding trails that are faint, hidden, or even days old.

But this mission isn't just about learning, it's about **action**. You'll start observing your dog like a true scent detective, watching for zigzags, pauses, and head tilts that reveal how they process scent in real time. Then, you'll use your new scent smarts to design clever hiding spots and set up thrilling search games.

Your challenge: teach your dog to track down a high-value treat like a piece of cheese. You'll create safe, exciting scent trails, guide your dog through the search, and celebrate every successful find. These games are fun, easy to set up, and packed with learning. And they're your next step toward becoming a scent detection duo.

By the end of this chapter, you'll understand how scent behaves, how your dog's nose interprets it, and how to build your own sniffing missions from scratch. You'll also earn your **Super Sniffer Science Scout** badge – a symbol of curiosity, clever thinking, and teamwork with your canine partner.

So grab your field journal, prep your treats, and stay alert. Dr. Whiff may send a Mystery Alert at any moment, and you'll want to be ready before the Crumb Bandit strikes again. Your mission starts now!

The Science of Canine Smell: Understanding the Sniffing Machine

Your dog's nose isn't just for sniffing – it's a high-tech scent detector built for mystery-solving missions. While humans rely mostly on sight, dogs navigate the world through smell. And they're not just good at it, they're phenomenal. With up to 300 million scent receptors (compared to our measly 6 million), dogs can detect smells up to 10,000 times better than we can. That's like smelling one cookie crumb in a bakery the size of a city block!

Why Your Dog's Nose is Wet

Inside your dog's nose is a twisty maze of thin, curled bones called **turbinates**. These bones are covered in millions of scent-sensing cells and give your dog's nose a huge surface area – kind of like unfolding a giant sponge from inside a tiny space! The more surface area there is, the more scent particles your dog can catch and sniff.

But here's the cool part: your dog's nose is **wet on purpose**. That moisture isn't just slobber – it's made by special glands that produce **mucus**. This sticky layer helps trap scent particles from the air, like flypaper for smells. A wet nose also helps cool the air as it flows through, keeping your dog's sniffer working smoothly even during rapid sniffing.

So when your dog sniffs, scent particles stick to the moist surface and travel through the turbinates, where they get sorted and sent to the brain. It's like a scent-sorting super highway – and it all starts with that amazing wet nose!

Sniffing in Stereo

Dogs don't just sniff once and move on. They sniff **rapidly**, up to five times per second, gathering clues from every angle (try to see how many times you can sniff in one second!). Even cooler? They can sniff and breathe at the same time. Their nose splits incoming air into two paths: one for breathing, one for smelling. That means they never miss a whiff, even mid-breath.

And here's where things get really clever: dogs sniff **in stereo**. Each nostril works independently, helping them detect which direction a scent is coming from. If it's stronger on the left, they turn left. Stronger on the right? You guessed it – they pivot right. It's like having a built-in scent GPS.

Those little slits on the sides of their nose? They're not just decorative. When a dog exhales, air flows out through those slits, stirring up more scent particles and pulling them in, like stirring soup to release all the delicious smells.

The Secret Sensor

Hidden in the roof of your dog's mouth is a bonus scent detector: the **vomeronasal organ** (say it like VOH-muh-roh-NAY-zuhl – how many times can you say this in a row?). This special sensor picks up chemical messages called pheromones – clues about how other animals are feeling, who's nearby, or even if someone's sick. When your dog lifts their lip or makes a funny face after sniffing something, they're activating this organ to gather extra intel.

Every Sniff Tells a Story

Every time your dog stops to sniff, they're reading an invisible story. That patch of grass? It might hold clues about a dog who walked by earlier, a bird that landed briefly, or a snack crumb dropped days ago. To your dog, every scent trail is packed with information – who was here, what they were doing, and how long ago they left. It's like a scent-powered time machine!

Super Sniffer Science: The Brainpower Behind the Nose

Your dog's nose isn't just powerful, it's connected to a scent-sorting supercomputer in their brain. When scent particles enter the nose, they're sent straight to the **olfactory bulb**, a part of the brain that's 40 times bigger in dogs than in humans (compared to brain size). This bulb decodes what the smell is, where it came from, and whether it's familiar or new.

Even cooler? The olfactory bulb is linked to the **limbic system**, which handles emotions and memories. That's why smells can trigger excitement, caution, or curiosity in your dog. If they sniff a toy they haven't seen in months, they might light up with recognition – because their brain remembers the scent! Dogs can store scent memories for years. That means your dog might remember the scent of a friend from the park, a favorite treat, or even a trail they followed ages ago. Their nose isn't just sniffing – it's storytelling and remembering.

Sniffing Styles and Scent Sorting

Dogs don't just smell one thing at a time. Their brains can **separate and identify multiple scents** in a single sniff. So when your dog sniffs a patch of grass, they might detect a rabbit trail, a snack crumb, and a flower, all at once. This skill is called **olfactory discrimination**, and it's what makes scent games so exciting. Even if you hide a treat among other smells, your dog can still find the right scent.

And just like detectives have different methods, dogs have different **sniffing styles**. Some sniff low and steady, nose glued to the ground. Others bounce around, zigzagging like they're chasing invisible clues. Some pause and scan, using both nose and eyes to solve puzzles. You might even notice your dog spiraling around a scent source, narrowing in like a pro.

Learning your dog's sniffing style helps you support them during missions. Whether they're a tracker, a bouncer, or a spiral sniffer, their style is part of their superpower, and part of what makes your team unique.

Now that you understand how your dog's nose works, you're one step closer to becoming a true Sniff Squad Detective. In the missions ahead, you'll learn how to harness these superpowers through training, teamwork, and a whole lot of sniff-tastic fun. And speaking of missions… your next mystery is about to begin. Get ready to dive into another **Super Sniffer Mystery** – this one might just involve a trail of crumbs, a missing snack, and a very sneaky suspect!

Super Sniffer Mystery
The Case of the Missing Cheese

Incoming Mystery Alert!:

Something cheesy is going on at Sniff Squad HQ. A delicious piece of cheese has mysteriously vanished from the kitchen counter. Did it roll under the couch? Was it hidden by a clever agent for training? Or... was it the Crumb Bandit?

Sniff Squad Orders:

Help your dog use their super sniffer to locate the missing cheese and crack the case wide open. Keep it simple, keep it fun, and get ready to celebrate every sniff along the way.

Mission Kit Checklist:

- ☐ A small piece of strong-smelling cheese
- ☐ 3-5 identical containers (plastic cups, small boxes, or bowls)
- ☐ A quiet indoor space with minimal distractions
- ☐ A leash or harness (optional for guidance)
- ☐ Your Field Journal to record your dog's search style, results and patterns of behavior

Parent Tips for Younger Recruits:

For younger recruits, take turns hiding the cheese, ensure the challenge isn't too hard or too easy, use pet-friendly reward treats and cheer every sniff!

Sniff Instructions:

1. Choose your search zone: Pick a quiet room with a clear floor. Have your dog sit a few feet away and stay.
2. Prepare the scent: Place the cheese under one of the containers. Leave the others empty.
3. Let your dog watch you hide the cheese.
4. Cue the search: Use your search phrase (e.g. "Find it!" or "Search!") and allow your dog to sniff the containers.
5. Watch and learn: Observe how your dog investigates—do they sniff, paw, nudge, or sit near the correct container?
6. Celebrate the find: When they locate the cheese, reward with whatever motivates your dog the most (treat, play or praise – or all three!).
7. Work your way through each mystery level below, in order!

Level 1

Rookie Sniffer

- Let your dog watch you hide the cheese under one of the containers.
- Keep the search area small and quiet.
- Use containers with no lids or covers, so it's easy for your dog to trace the smell.

Level 2

Jnr Detective

- Hide the cheese while your dog is in another room.
- Move the containers around and mix them up before the search begins.
- Cover the containers with lids, a towel or cloth.

Level 3

Master Sleuth

- Add decoy scents (e.g. a cotton ball with a drop of vanilla) in one of the other containers.
- Use more containers and space them farther apart.
- Wait 1–2 mins after hiding the cheese.

Badge Readiness Checklist

Nice work, Recruit! You and your canine partner have just solved your very first scent case. Your teamwork, timing, and nose power are seriously impressive. But before you can officially claim your **Super Sniffer Science Scout** badge, there are a few final tasks to complete. These last steps will fine-tune your skills and prove you're ready to rise through the Sniff Squad ranks.

I'm ready!

- ❏ I can explain how my dog's wet nose helps trap smells.
- ❏ I understand how turbinates give more sniffing surface.
- ❏ I can explain how each nostril works on its own and how one can be used for familiar smells and one for new smells.
- ❏ I know how the olfactory bulb decodes scent and stores memories, so my dog never forgets a scent.
- ❏ I can describe how dogs sort mixed smells.
- ❏ I've recorded how my dog sniffs during searches and their different search styles in my Field Journal.
- ❏ I believe every sniff reveals hidden clues and stories

Badge Unlocked: Super Sniffer Science Scout!

Congratulations, Recruit! You've officially earned your **Super Sniffer Science Scout** badge. You now understand how your dog's nose works, how they remember scents and why they are superheroes at sniffing. With this badge, you're ready to learn about how scent moves like a ghost.

Mission Debrief: Operation Follow Your Nose Complete!

Recruit, HQ is buzzing, and it's all because of YOU.

You've cracked another Super Sniffer Mystery wide open, uncovering the science behind your dog's **nose-powered superpowers**. From scent-sorting cells to stereo sniffing and a brain built for decoding invisible clues, you now know exactly why your dog is a four-legged detective with turbo-charged tracking skills.

But this wasn't just a science lesson – it was your launchpad. You ran your first scent mission, played sniff-tastic games, and watched your dog come alive with curiosity and focus. And yes… you solved the case. The missing cheese? Recovered. The Crumb Bandit? Out-sniffed and outsmarted. For now.

You've officially earned your **Super Sniffer Science Scout** badge, proving you've got the brains, bravery, and bond to sniff out the truth. You're not just a recruit anymore, you're a rising star in the Sniff Squad, and the Crumb Bandit knows it.

Next up: you'll unlock the secrets of how scent travels invisibly through air, and how wind and weather change the game.

So grab your **field journal**, prep your treats, and tighten your leash, your next mystery is just around the corner. Let's sniff smart, lead strong, and keep the crumbs where they belong.

Chapter Four

Ghost Scent Trails
Tracking the Invisible

E**YES SHARP, RECRUIT!** You've unlocked the power of the Super Sniffer – your dog's nose is a scent radar in motion. Now it's time to level up. Scent doesn't sit still – it drifts, twists, and hides like a ghost. In this mission, you'll learn to read the air, track the invisible, and think like a true scent detective.

Ready to chase what can't be seen? Let's go!

Mission #4: Operation Ghost Scent

Heads up Recruit, we've just received a new transmission from Dr. Whiff at HQ. The air is shifting. Reports of vanishing scent trails and phantom smells are coming in from all over. Something strange is happening, and your dog's nose isn't the only one that has noticed.

This mission is unlike anything you've faced before. You're about to enter the world of **ghost scents** – those invisible, drifting clues that swirl through wind, cling to cool surfaces, and vanish without warning. They're the whispers of the scent world, and only a trained scent detective can track them.

Your objective: learn how scent moves through the **environment**. Understand how wind, weather, and terrain shape the invisible trails your dog follows. This time, you won't be chasing treats, you'll be chasing shadows.

Stay sharp. Stay curious. The ghost scents are out there… and they're waiting to be found!

How Scent Travels: Wind, Weather and Scent Trails

Have you ever noticed how your dog's nose twitches and moves when they catch an interesting smell? Before you start hiding treats in the garden or setting up search games in your home, there's something every Sniff Squad Recruit should know: scent doesn't sit still. **It moves**. It floats, sticks, swirls, and sometimes disappears altogether. And your dog's nose is constantly reading these **invisible clues** – like a detective scanning a crime scene that only they can smell.

You'll learn to train in all kinds of weather later in the book, but it's helpful to start noticing how scent behaves now. That way, you'll understand what your dog is reacting to, so you can set up smarter, safer missions from the very beginning.

Wind: The Invisible Trail Maker

Imagine you're standing in your backyard. You've just hidden a treat behind a bush, and the wind starts to blow. That treat's smell doesn't stay put – it travels! The wind picks it up and spreads it out in a triangle shape called a **scent cone**. Your dog doesn't just run straight to the treat, they zigzag through the scent cone, sniffing left and right like they're chasing a ghost. That's why they look so wiggly when they're tracking – they're following the scent trail, not just guessing.

If you want to help your dog catch the scent faster, try standing so the wind is blowing from the treat toward your dog (that's what we mean when we say being "downwind" of the treat). That way, the smell reaches them right away. And if the wind is strong, hiding the treat behind a bush or wall can help trap the scent in one spot, like a little scent puddle waiting to be discovered.

Temperature and Humidity: Sticky or Slippery?

Scent doesn't just move with the wind, it also reacts to the air around it. On hot days, scent particles rise into the air like steam from a hot chocolate. Your dog might sniff the breeze, lifting their nose to catch the scent floating above. On cooler days, scent stays low to the ground, and your dog's nose will hover just above the surface, sweeping back and forth like a radar.

Early mornings are awesome for training because the cool air keeps scent close to the ground. It's like laying out a trail of invisible breadcrumbs that your dog can follow step by step.

Humidity - how damp the air is – makes a big difference too. When the air is moist, scent sticks to surfaces like grass, leaves, and even your shoes. That makes it easier for your dog to track. But when the air is dry, scent disappears faster, like steam vanishing from a hot cup of tea. After a light rain or on misty mornings, scent tends to hang around longer, creating stronger trails for your dog to follow.

So if it's dry and sunny, use super smelly treats like cheese or liver to help your dog stay focused. And if it's damp or cool, try hiding treats under leaves or near damp logs. Those spots hold scent like magnets!

Terrain: The Scent Playground

Now let's talk about the ground beneath your feet. The shape of the land – hills, valleys, trees, fences, and even furniture, can change how scent moves. These obstacles bounce scent around, trap it in corners, or swirl it into little scent whirlpools called **eddy currents**. Indoors, things like fans, heaters, and open windows do the same thing. Your dog learns to sniff high and low, around edges and under tables, piecing together the puzzle of where the scent has settled.

Watch your dog closely when they sniff around furniture or bushes. They're not just being curious, they're checking for **scent pools** where smells have gathered. Try hiding treats in tricky spots like behind a chair leg or under a cushion and see how your dog investigates. You'll start to notice their search patterns: the pause, the head tilt, the deep sniff. That's their way of saying, "I'm onto something!

Super Sniffer Mystery
The Trail of the Ghost Bandit

Incoming Mystery Alert!:

Dr Whiff has reported that a trail of crumbs has been spotted winding through Sniff Squad HQ. Someone—or something—has been sneaking snacks again. Was it the Crumb Bandit? Or a ghostly presence leading you on a dead-end chase?

Sniff Squad Orders:

Your mission is to guide your dog through a fun, scent-filled search using their super sniffer to track down hidden clues. Stay curious, stay patient, and celebrate every tail-wagging discovery!

Mission Kit Checklist:

- ☐ 5–10 small, smelly treats (soft and crumbly)
- ☐ A quiet indoor space with a clear floor
- ☐ A leash or harness (optional for guidance)
- ☐ Your field journal to record your dog's tracking style and sniff approach
- ☐ Optional: cushions or furniture to create gentle obstacles

Parent Tips for Younger Recruits:

Start simple with smelly treats and short trails. Let kids observe sniffing styles, cheer every effort, adjust difficulty if needed.

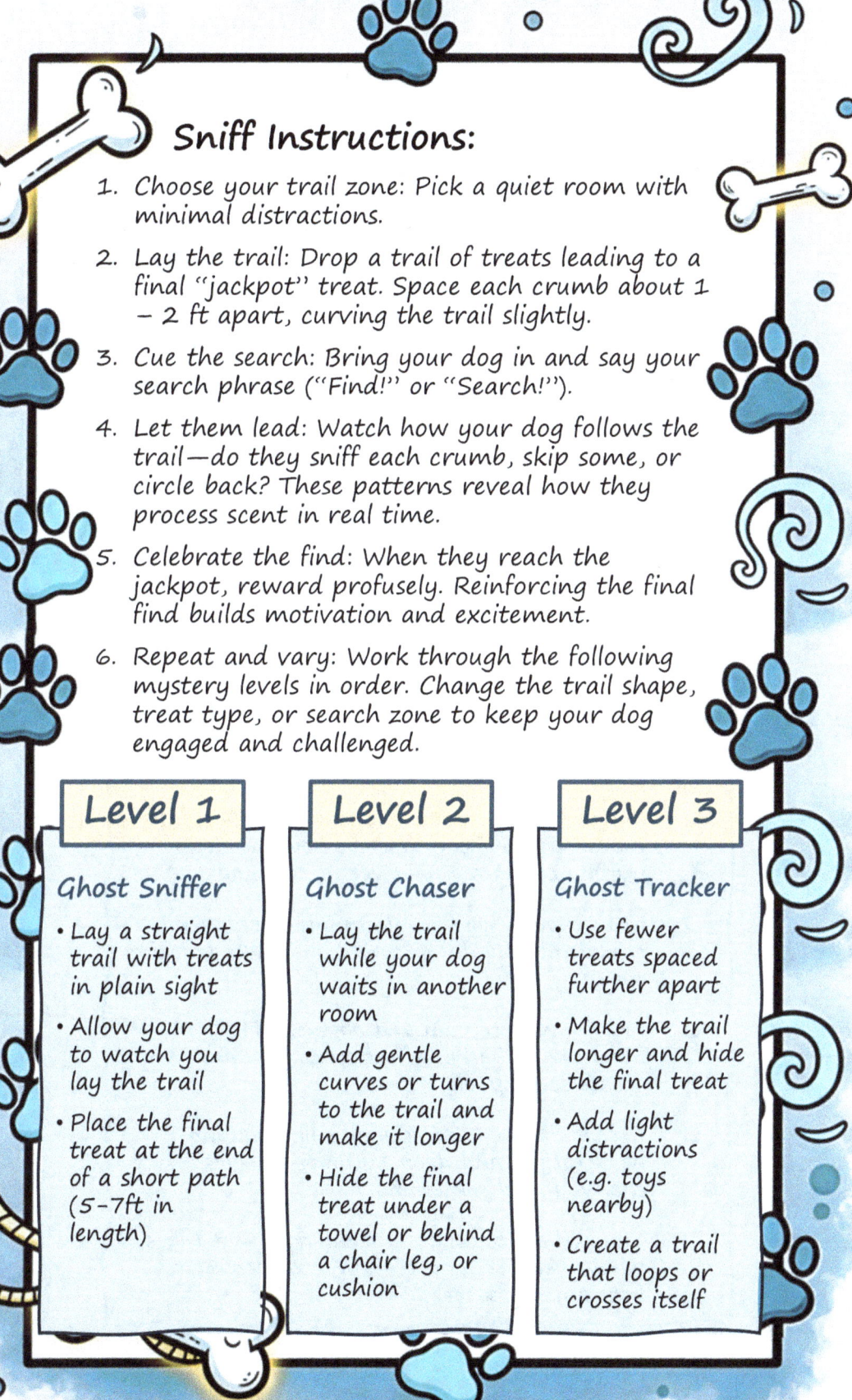

Sniff Instructions:

1. **Choose your trail zone:** Pick a quiet room with minimal distractions.
2. **Lay the trail:** Drop a trail of treats leading to a final "jackpot" treat. Space each crumb about 1 – 2 ft apart, curving the trail slightly.
3. **Cue the search:** Bring your dog in and say your search phrase ("Find!" or "Search!").
4. **Let them lead:** Watch how your dog follows the trail—do they sniff each crumb, skip some, or circle back? These patterns reveal how they process scent in real time.
5. **Celebrate the find:** When they reach the jackpot, reward profusely. Reinforcing the final find builds motivation and excitement.
6. **Repeat and vary:** Work through the following mystery levels in order. Change the trail shape, treat type, or search zone to keep your dog engaged and challenged.

Level 1
Ghost Sniffer
- Lay a straight trail with treats in plain sight
- Allow your dog to watch you lay the trail
- Place the final treat at the end of a short path (5-7ft in length)

Level 2
Ghost Chaser
- Lay the trail while your dog waits in another room
- Add gentle curves or turns to the trail and make it longer
- Hide the final treat under a towel or behind a chair leg, or cushion

Level 3
Ghost Tracker
- Use fewer treats spaced further apart
- Make the trail longer and hide the final treat
- Add light distractions (e.g. toys nearby)
- Create a trail that loops or crosses itself

Badge Readiness Checklist

Recruit, you've just completed one of HQ's trickiest missions – tracking a ghostly bandit using invisible scent trails. You learned how scent travels and fades, how to leave ghostly crumb paths, and how to guide your dog through a search where the clues are hidden in the air. Now it's time to prove you're ready to earn your **Ghost Scent Decoder** badge. Tick off each skill below to show you've mastered the art of the invisible scents – and that you and your dog are ready for whatever comes next.

I'm ready!

- ❑ I can explain what a scent cone is and how my dog moves through it when tracking.
- ❑ I know why zigzagging is part of their search pattern and what it reveals about scent behavior.
- ❑ I understand how temperature affects scent movement and can describe how my dog's sniffing changes on hot versus cool days.
- ❑ I can explain how humidity influences scent trails and why damp conditions make tracking easier.
- ❑ I notice how terrain and obstacles like furniture or bushes affect scent flow and create scent pools.
- ❑ I recognize my dog's signals—like pausing, head tilting, and deep sniffing—as clues they've found something.
- ❑ I know how to set up a scent trail that takes wind, weather, and terrain into account to help my dog succeed.

Badge Unlocked: Ghost Scent Decoder!

Congratulations Recruit – the Ghost Scent Decoder badge marks your mastery of the invisible. You've learned how scent drifts through wind, clings to cool surfaces, and pools in hidden corners – just like a ghost leaving clues behind. With this badge, you've proven you can read the air, spot scent traps, and understand how your dog tracks what others can't even see. You're officially one step closer to becoming a fully-fledged scent detective.

Mission Debrief: Operation Ghost Scent Complete!

Well done, Recruit. You've officially cracked one of the trickiest mysteries in scent science, and earned your **Ghost Scent Decoder** badge.

This mission took you deep into the invisible world of scent movement. You discovered how wind sculpts scent into cones, how temperature lifts or grounds it, and how humidity can either anchor a trail or make it vanish like a ghost. You learned to read the environment like a seasoned tracker, watching how scent pools behind furniture, swirls in eddy currents, and clings to damp leaves or vanishes in dry air.

You didn't just study the science, you used it. You set up smarter trails and watched your dog zigzag, pause, and sniff with purpose. You saw first-hand how scent behaves like a living thing, slipping through cracks, bouncing off walls, and hiding in plain sight.

And when the Crumb Bandit tried to throw you off with a twisted trail through HQ, you stayed sharp. You trusted your dog's nose, adapted to the shifting scent-scape, and solved the mystery with teamwork and tenacity.

Dr. Whiff is impressed! The Crumb Bandit? Not so much.

Badge unlocked. Mission complete. But, stay alert – ghost trails are everywhere, and the next mystery could be swirling in the air already.

Chapter Five

Smell & Tell
Unlocking Scent Articles

YOU'VE EARNED YOUR NEXT **challenge, Recruit.** You've completed your basic training – sniffing out treats, following simple trails – but those were just warm-ups. You've proven you can follow the scent. Now it's time to follow the story. Dr. Whiff and Sniff Squad HQ are activating your next level of scent detective work. This chapter unlocks the secrets of **scent detection articles** – special objects that carry a unique smell and launch real search missions. These aren't just socks, toys, or cookie crumbs. They're clues. Evidence. The first whiff of a mystery waiting to be solved.

Mission #5: Operation Smell and Tell

Recruit, report to HQ immediately! Dr. Whiff has issued a high-priority mission following a troubling new sighting. Late last night, surveillance picked up a trail of cookie crumbs snaking from the snack stash to a dead end – no exit, no explanation. Just a scatter of tiny pawprints, muffin bits in the mailbox, and a banana peel tucked behind the garden gnome. And then… the sock. Crumb-covered. Suspiciously placed. Reeking of mischief.

This isn't random. It's a pattern. A calling card. The Crumb Bandit is escalating, and we need to sharpen our scent detection skills before the trail goes cold.

Your mission: learn the art of **scent detection articles**. These aren't just everyday objects, they're evidence. Socks, toys, scraps, and crumbs become launchpads for real search operations. You'll train your dog to sniff the article, lock onto its unique **scent signature**, and track it like a seasoned Sniff Squad sleuth.

Dr. Whiff has authorized a full training protocol. Watch closely as your dog shifts into "scent mode" – every pause, nose twitch, and tail wag is a clue.

You're not just playing games anymore. You're decoding mysteries, and a Mystery Alert is bound to arrive any second!

This is the foundation of real-world tracking, search-and-rescue, and forensic scentwork. And it's the only way we'll ever catch The Crumb Bandit.

We're levelling up now, so remember: every great detective team starts small. Your dog learns at their own pace, and every sniff is progress. Celebrate the effort. Cheer the tiny wins. With practice, patience, and praise, you and your canine partner will become unstoppable.

This sock is just the beginning. Grab your gear, Recruit, let's get to work!

A Detective's First Clue

Every great detective needs a clue to get started – and for scent detectives, that clue is **smell**. But not just any smell. Dogs need something specific to sniff, something that carries the scent of the person or thing they're trying to find. That special object is called a **scent article**.

When sniffing out humans, a scent article is anything that holds a person's unique smell. It might be a sock, a hat, a toy, a pillowcase, or even a cookie crumb. That's right – your body leaves behind tiny scent particles on everything you touch. These particles are made of skin cells, sweat, oils, and even the things you eat. To humans, they're invisible. But to dogs, they're like glowing arrows pointing the way.

Every person has their own **scent signature** – like a fingerprint made of smell. And your dog's nose is built to read it. In fact, dogs brains are wired to decode **scent trails**, compare smells, and follow them to the source. That's why scent articles are so important – they give your dog a clear target to track.

Why do we use scent articles?

Recruit, this is big. If you want to become a top-level scent detective, you need to understand the power of a scent article. It might look like an ordinary object – a cap, a scarf, a sock – but to your dog, it's a smell-packed clue. A scent article carries the unique scent of the person, pet, or object you're trying to find. It's like giving your dog a whiff of the mystery before the search begins.

Working dogs use scent articles in all kinds of amazing ways. Search and rescue dogs can sniff a missing person's shirt or pillowcase and track them through forests, mountains, or even after natural disasters. These dogs have found lost hikers, kids who've wandered off, and people trapped under rubble, just by following the scent from one item.

Police dogs use scent articles to chase down suspects or find stolen items. If someone breaks into a house and leaves behind a glove, that glove becomes the key to the chase. The dog sniffs it, locks onto the scent, and follows the trail, even if the person tries to hide or escape.

Medical detection dogs use scent articles to help doctors. They can sniff someone's breath or clothing and detect illnesses like cancer, diabetes, or even COVID-19. That's right, some dogs can smell when someone is sick!

Wildlife conservation dogs use scent articles to help scientists protect animals. They can sniff out endangered species like koalas or hairy-nosed wombats, or track down invasive pests like cane toads or foxes. These dogs help save habitats and keep ecosystems healthy, all by following scent clues.

And here's the part that's super cool for you: scent articles can help your dog find things around the house too. Imagine Mum or Dad losing their car keys again. You hand your dog a keychain they've touched, your dog sniffs it, locks onto the scent, and starts searching. Under the couch? Behind the curtains? In the laundry basket? Your dog becomes a real-life finder of lost things. Glasses, toys, phones, even a missing sock. Your dog can learn to track them all.

Using scent articles teaches your dog to focus on one specific smell, even when there are lots of other smells around. It's like tuning into the right radio station in a sea of static. This skill is the foundation of real scent detection – and it's what separates a casual sniffer from a certified Sniff Squad Detective.

So whether you're solving snack-based crimes, helping someone find their missing pet, or tracking down a trail left by the Crumb Bandit, scent articles are your starting point. They're the first clue in every great mystery, and your dog's nose is ready to follow it.

How dogs use scent articles: From sniff to source

When your dog is handed a scent article, like a sock, a toy, or a snack wrapper, they're not just sniffing it for fun. They're launching into a full-on detective mission, using their super-powered nose to track down the source of that smell. Let's follow the journey from the very first sniff to the final discovery.

It all begins with the **Sniff and Lock-On** phase. Your dog takes a deep sniff of the scent article, and their brain instantly starts decoding the smell. It's like reading a recipe made of invisible ingredients: skin cells, sweat, shampoo, laundry detergent, maybe even cookie crumbs from snack time. Every scent article is packed with clues, and your dog's nose can separate and remember each one. They're building a scent "picture" of the person or object, like a smell-based fingerprint. Once they've locked onto that scent, they're ready to search.

Next comes the **Search and Compare** phase. Your dog begins moving through the area, sniffing the air, the ground, and anything nearby; walls, furniture, plants, even shoes left by the door. Their nose is constantly asking, "Does this match the scent article? Is this close? Is this stronger?" Dogs don't just sniff once and go, they sniff, compare, re-check, and adjust as they move. Their brain is running a nonstop scent scan, looking for anything that matches the smell they memorized.

If the scent is fresh, your dog may enter the **Follow the Trail** phase. As the person or object moved through the space, they left behind tiny scent particles like invisible breadcrumbs. These particles can stick to grass, carpet, furniture, or even float in the air. Your dog follows this trail, adjusting their path based on how strong or weak the scent becomes. If the trail gets faint, they might zigzag, circle back, or pause to re-scan the area.

Finally, your dog **Finds the Source**. This is the moment they track the scent to its origin. Maybe it's a person hiding behind a couch, a sock tucked under a blanket, or a toy buried in the laundry basket. Your dog will give a signal – it might be a tail wag, a sit, a bark, or just a proud look that says, "I found it!" It's their way of saying, "Mission complete."

This entire process, from sniff to source, is what makes scent detection so powerful. Your dog isn't just guessing. They're using science, memory, and instinct to solve a mystery. And with practice, they'll get faster, sharper, and more confident with every search.

Super Sniffer Mystery
The Crumb-Covered Sock

Incoming Mystery Alert!:

Recruits, listen up! HQ have just issued an official mystery alert following last night's suspicious activity. The Crumb Bandit has struck again and Dr Whiff has confirmed the crumb-covered sock is no ordinary laundry casualty. It's a clue!

Sniff Squad Orders:

Your mission? Focus on the sock. Study it. Sniff it. Use it as your scent article to launch a full-scale search. Somewhere out there, the matching sock is hiding—and it may lead us straight to the Bandit's hideout.

Mission Kit Checklist:

- ☐ One smelly sock with cookie crumbs
- ☐ One matching smelly sock with crumbs (target) hidden in the search zone
- ☐ High-value treats or favorite toy for reward
- ☐ A quiet indoor or outdoor space with fun hiding spots (blankets, boxes, cushions)
- ☐ Your field journal to record sniffing styles & success

Parent Tips for Younger Recruits:

Let kids use their smelly socks to build excitement and assist with covering in crumbs. Use a safe outdoor area if concerned about mess.

Sniff Instructions:

1. **Choose your trail zone:** Pick a quiet area with minimal distractions, either indoor or outdoor.
2. **Hide the target (matching sock):** At first, put the target in view of your dog (e.g. several feet away), but hide it out of sight while your dog is not watching, for levels 2 and 3.
3. **Sniff the clue:** Let your dog smell the crumb-covered sock to lock onto the scent.
4. **Cue the search:** Give your dog the search phrase ("Find!" or "Search!"). Make sure this is the same cue you've been using for all the other scent searches so your dog learns the command.
5. **Let your dog lead** and celebrate the find once they have found the matching sock.
6. **Repeat and vary:** Work through each of the following mystery levels in order. Change the trail shape, treat type, or search zone to keep your dog engaged and challenged.

Level 1

Sock Sniffer

- Let your dog sniff the crumb-covered sock (scent article)
- Place the target sock in plain view close by
- Use your search cue & cheer when your dog finds the matching sock!

Level 2

Crumb Trail

- Create a trail of cookie crumbs from your starting point
- Hide the target sock at the end of the trail
- Cue your search & reward success when your dog finds the matching sock!

Level 3

Hidden Sock

- Let your dog sniff the scent article
- Hide the matching sock under a blanket, behind a cushion, or inside a box
- Use your search cue & reward success when your dog finds the sock!

Badge Readiness Checklist

Well done, Recruit! You've officially cracked using scent articles to launch a real search. You tracked down the missing crumb-covered sock left behind by the Crumb Bandit, and that means you're ready for bigger missions. This skill opens up a whole new world of scent detection. From now on, every Sniff Squad mission will begin with a scent clue – whether it's a missing toy, a lost sock, or a suspicious snack trail. You and your canine partner now know how to follow a specific smell all the way to its source. You're not just in training anymore. You're in the big league!

I'm ready!

- ☐ I know what a scent article is and how it helps my dog know what to search for.
- ☐ I can name a few everyday items that could be used as scent articles—like socks, toys, or snack wrappers.
- ☐ I understand that scent articles carry a special smell that my dog can follow.
- ☐ I've seen how my dog sniffs the scent article before starting the search.
- ☐ I noticed how my dog compares smells while searching—sniffing the ground, air, and nearby things.
- ☐ I know that scent particles can stick to surfaces or float in the air, and my dog can follow them.
- ☐ I helped my dog use a scent article to find the missing crumb-covered sock left by the Crumb Bandit!

Badge Unlocked: Scent Article Agent!

Boom! You did it, Agent! You've earned your **Scent Article Agent** badge. Proof that you and your dog can sniff a clue and chase it down like true scent detectives. From socks to snack wrappers, you know how to turn everyday stuff into mystery-solving magic. This is your first step into real tracking missions. Watch out Crumb Bandit!

Mission Debrief: Operation Smell and Tell Complete!

Whoa Recruit, you crushed it! You sniffed, searched, and sleuthed your way through one of the most important skills in scent detection – using a scent article to launch a mission. And guess what? You didn't just learn it… you *nailed* it. That crumb-covered sock didn't stand a chance.

You now know how to pick the perfect **scent clue**, help your dog lock onto the smell, and follow the trail like a real Sniff Squad Detective. You've seen how scent particles stick to surfaces, float through the air, and lead straight to the source. You've watched your dog compare smells, zigzag through the search zone, and give the signal when the mystery was cracked. That's serious nosework.

And now? You've officially earned your **Scent Article Agent** badge. That means you're no longer just training – you're tracking. Every future mission will start with a scent article, and you've got the skills to turn everyday objects into top-level clues.

But don't get too comfy, Agent. The Crumb Bandit is still out there, and the mysteries ahead are about to get wilder, trickier, and way more delicious. You've passed the first big test – but to become a fully certified Sniff Squad Detective, you'll need to level up your skills, sharpen your instincts, and stay one sniff ahead.

Next chapter? Bigger clues. Bolder missions. And a trail that might just lead us straight into the Bandit's lair.

Get ready. The scent saga continues…

Chapter Six

Lead Like a Legend
How to be the Brain Behind the Sniff

YOU NAILED YOUR LAST mission and earned your **Scent Article Agent** badge - now it's time to level up. This challenge isn't just about sniffing; it's about **leading**. Your dog's nose is the superpower, but you're the commander. Move with purpose, read the signals, and guide like a pro…

Mission #6: Operation Cold Trail

Recruit, we've received an incoming alert from Dr. Whiff – HQ just got hit! At 0600 hours, a trail of cookie crumbs was discovered in the Academy's training yard. But this time, there was no snack, no sock… just a giant question mark made of crumbs and a challenge on a piece of paper: *"Can you lead when the trail goes cold?"*

This isn't just a test of your dog's nose – it's a test of *you*. The Crumb Bandit is getting clever, and that means we need to get sharper. Your dog may be the lead sniffer, but you are in charge of the mission. You launch the search. You guide the action. You read the clues in real time – and you keep your cool when things get confusing.

This chapter is all about **leading with purpose**. You'll learn how to give a clear search cue, move with purpose, and support your dog like a coach – not a boss. You'll practice reading sniff signals, adjusting your body language, and celebrating every win with style. But more importantly, you'll build **emotional intelligence**: staying calm when you're excited or frustrated, understanding your dog's feelings, and working with your canine as a team.

Because great handlers don't just give commands – they build trust, understand how their dog thinks, and know how to turn a mystery into a mission.

Your goal is to become a **confident** handler who can lead the search, support your dog, and decode the mystery – no matter what the Crumb Bandit throws your way. The trail may be confusing. The clues may be sneaky. But with kindness, focus, and leadership, you've got what it takes.

The mission begins now. Let's **lead like legends!**

The Brain Behind the Sniff

Leading like a legend means stepping into your role as mission commander. You're the one who launches the search, guides the action, and keeps the team focused when the trail gets twisty. And guess what? Your dog is watching you – closely. If you're calm and confident, they feel safe and ready to sniff like a superstar. If you're tense or frustrated, they get confused and can lose focus.

That's why your **energy**, your attitude, and your **leadership** matter. When you lead with trust, clarity, and kindness, your dog learns faster, searches better, and feels proud to be part of your team. You're building a bond, solving mysteries, and showing the Crumb Bandit that this squad means business.

Cue Like You Mean It

Your **search cue** is your launch button. It's the phrase that tells your dog, "Let's go!" But it's not just about the words – it's about **how you say them**.

A strong, clear cue like "Search!" or "Find it!" helps your dog know it's game on.

Your **body language** matters too. Dogs are experts at reading your **tone and posture**. If you're unsure, they'll hesitate. If you're clear and upbeat, they'll charge ahead with confidence.

So stand tall. Point with purpose. Move like a leader – not like someone who just got lost in the cereal aisle. When you cue with confidence, your dog knows it's time to sniff like a superstar.

Keep Your Cool

Before you launch any mission, check in with your own **feelings**. Are you feeling excited? Nervous? A little frustrated because your dog just sniffed a sandwich instead of the sock?

Here's the thing: your dog can feel what **you're feeling**. If you're anxious, they get tense. If you're calm and confident, they relax and focus. That's why great handlers learn to notice their own emotions, how their emotions affect their dogs behavior, and stay cool and confident under pressure.

Take a deep breath. Shake out your shoulders. You've got this. When you stay steady, your dog feels safe – and that's when the real teamwork begins.

Decode Your Dog

Your dog is talking to you all the time – just not with words. A sudden pause? A tail wag? A zig-zag sniff pattern? These are all clues that your dog is communicating with you!

Your job is to notice when your dog is confident, curious, or confused. If they seem stuck, offer gentle **encouragement**. If they're locked in and sniffing like a pro, cheer them on!

When you understand what your dog is feeling, you can support them better – and that builds trust. Learning to read your dog's signals is like unlocking a **secret language**. And once you know it, your missions get way more awesome.

Be a Sniff Squad Team

Here's the deal: you both have a job to do – your dog leads with their nose and you lead the mission. That means working **together**. You both need each other to crack the case. Don't yank, shout, or hover. Instead, guide with gentle movements, clear cues, and lots of encouragement. Let your dog do what they do best – sniff!

Dogs work best when they feel supported – not bossed around. If your dog veers off course, help them refocus. If they're doing great, let them roll! And when they find the target – celebrate like you just won the Sniff-lympics. High fives, happy dances, and treat showers are totally allowed.

When your dog feels like you're on their team – not just giving orders – they'll search harder, faster and with more joy.

Lead with Kindness

Sometimes the trail goes cold. Sometimes your dog sniffs a sandwich instead of the sock. Sometimes your little brother walks through the scent zone wearing peanut butter-covered socks. Missions can get messy.

But great handlers stay cool. They cheer when things go well, stay **kind** when things go sideways, and treat everyone – dogs, friends, family – with respect.

Dogs (and people!) learn best when they feel **safe, respected, and encouraged**. When you lead with kindness, your dog learns to trust you – even when things get tricky. That's what makes you a true Sniff Squad leader.

Log It Like a Legend

Every mission teaches you something – if you take the time to notice. That's why your **field journal** is so important. After each search, jot down what worked, what didn't, and how you felt.

Did your cue work? Did your dog get distracted? Did you stay calm when the sock went missing? How did you stay calm? These notes help you grow and improve.

When you reflect on your progress, you become a smarter, stronger, more thoughtful leader – and your dog becomes a better teammate too.

Super Sniffer Mystery
Operation Cold Trail

Incoming Mystery Alert!:

At last, the Alert we were expecting has dropped! The Crumb Bandit's "question mark" has a trail of old crumbs scattered behind it across HQ. Each one faint, faded, and nearly impossible to detect. This isn't just a taunt—it's a test. Your dog's nose can still follow them, perhaps to the Bandit's lair - but only if you lead with focus and skill.

Sniff Squad Orders:

Lead your dog to follow a fading scent trail. This mission requires patience, focus, and teamwork. You'll need to stay calm, read your dog's signals, and offer just the right encouragement to keep your canine engaged and on track.

Mission Kit Checklist:

- ☐ One smelly sock with cookie crumbs
- ☐ One matching smelly sock with crumbs (target) hidden in the search zone
- ☐ Extra cookie crumbs (3-5 days old) for the trail
- ☐ A quiet outdoor space with fun hiding spots (bushes, trees, outdoor furniture, boxes)
- ☐ Your field journal to record sniffing styles & success

Parent Tips for Younger Recruits:

Supervise and encourage patience and gentle guidance, without giving away all the clues.

Sniff Instructions:

1. Pick a quiet outdoor area with no distractions and some good hiding spots.
2. Hide the target (matching sock) out of view and further away than usual.
3. Lay a trail of stale crumbs to the target. Space them out to make it harder.
4. Let your dog smell the scent article (crumb-covered sock) to lock onto the scent.
5. Confidently, give your dog the cue ("Find!" or "Search!"). Move with purpose and adjust your pace to match your dog's sniffing style.
6. Let your dog lead and gently guide them in the direction of the trail if they lose focus. Stay upbeat and encouraging as they sniff.
7. Repeat the same activity as you work through each level below.
8. Record your findings and your dog's sniff style in your Field Journal!

Level 1

Mood Master
- How do you feel leading up to the search?
- Is your energy helping or distracting your dog?
- Stay calm, confident and kind
- Coach your dog through to the end

Level 2

Sniff Watch
- What does each sniff, tail wag, or pause mean?
- Let your dog's signals guide your choice of what to do next
- Be a super spotter, not a guesser
- Record all your insights in your Field Journal

Level 3

Team Power
- How are you and your dog communicating?
- What is your dog telling you to do?
- Match your moves to your dog's rhythm
- Celebrate your success!

Badge Readiness Checklist

Nice work, Recruit! You've sniffed out clues, led with confidence, and cracked your first outdoor mystery. That's emotional intelligence in action – leading with focus, kindness, and trust. Now it's time to see if you're ready to earn your **Mission Leader** badge.

This badge isn't about barking orders – it's about being the kind of leader your dog can count on. Calm under pressure. Supportive in every win. Smart enough to know when to guide, when to cheer, and when to let the nose lead the way.

I'm ready!

- ☐ I checked in with my own feelings before the search and made sure my energy helped my dog stay calm and focused
- ☐ I used a clear, confident search cue so my dog knew exactly when the mission began
- ☐ I moved with purpose and stayed out of my dog's way so they could focus on sniffing
- ☐ I watched my dog's sniff signals and responded with encouragement or gentle guidance
- ☐ I supported my dog like a teammate, not a boss, and worked with them through the whole search
- ☐ I stayed kind and cool, even when the trail got tricky or things didn't go as planned
- ☐ I wrote down what worked, what didn't, and how I felt so I can keep growing as a handler

Badge Unlocked: Mission Leader!

You did it! You stayed calm, led with confidence, and coached your dog like a true Sniff Squad legend. By guiding the search with kindness, focus, and teamwork, you've officially earned your **Mission Leader** badge.

Mission Debrief: Operation Cold Trail Complete!

Whoa, Recruit – you crushed it! You've done more than complete a mission – you've levelled up as a true Sniff Squad leader.

You didn't just follow a trail. You led the way. You stayed calm when the scent faded, encouraged your dog when things got tricky, and tuned in to every tail flick, head tilt, and sniff pause like you were reading their mind. That's not magic – it's **emotional intelligence**, and it's what legendary leaders are made of.

You've learned to guide with **patience**, adapt with **confidence**, and celebrate every clue like a team. You and your dog? You're not just partners now – you're practically telepathic.

And as for the Crumb Bandit's challenge – *"Can you lead when the trail goes cold?"* – you've got your answer:

Yes. You can. And you did.

You've earned your **Mission Leader** badge – Dr. Whiff and the rest of HQ couldn't be prouder. But stay sharp. The Bandit's still out there, and he knows you're rising through the ranks.

The next mission is coming soon. Until then, keep leading with confidence – and keep that super sniffer nose ready.

Chapter Seven

The Great Indoor Drift
Where Scent Swirls and Secrets Hide

Time to gear up, Recruit! You cracked your first outdoor mystery and proved you can lead like a legend. But now you're stepping into a whole new challenge – **indoors**, where scent trails don't behave the way you expect. Inside, smells swirl through rooms, sneak under doors, and ride invisible air currents that twist and turn like a maze. Once you learn how scent moves through indoor spaces, you'll never look at your room the same way again. Let's drift in!

Mission #7: Operation Airwave

Hey there Recruit, another mission has just dropped from Dr. Whiff – and this one's urgent!

The Crumb Bandit has struck again. This time, he didn't just leave crumbs – he left chaos. Cookie-scented clues have been scattered across HQ in a pattern so bizarre, even the senior sniffers are stumped. Crumbs behind curtains. Trails under heaters. A banana skin floating on a ceiling fan. It's bold. It's baffling. It's… audacious.

Dr. Whiff suspects the Bandit is testing us again – using indoor **air currents** to hide his trail and confuse our best recruits. But we're not backing down. We're levelling up.

Your objective: Track the Bandit's scent trail through the twists and turns of indoor **airflow**. You'll need to guide your dog through **scent pools, dead zones, and vertical drift.** You'll use everything you learned about ghost scents and leadership to successfully decode this invisible trail.

This mission will stretch your brain, test your teamwork, and challenge you to stay cool when the clues get weird. If you crack it, you won't just level up – you'll outsmart the Crumb Bandit at his own game. He's getting sneakier, but so are you. And with every mission, you're sniffing closer to the moment we catch him red-handed (or crumb-handed!).

The Drift Zone: Cracking the Indoor Code

Microcurrents: The Invisible Waves

Here's something wild: every time you move, you stir the air. A single step, a swinging door, even your dog's tail wag creates tiny air shifts called **microcurrents**. You can't see them, but **scent molecules** ride those waves like surfers on a breeze.

Sometimes, these microcurrents help your dog catch a whiff of a hidden clue. Other times, they scatter the scent like confetti, making the trail harder to follow. That's why elite scent handlers learn to pause, observe, and reset when things get weird. If your dog suddenly loses the trail, ask yourself: did you just move? Did someone open a door? Did your dog do a happy spin?

In one mission, a recruit accidentally kicked a smelly sock across the room – and their dog started sniffing the ceiling. Why? Because the sock stirred up a scent pool that floated upward. The recruit had to stop, rethink, and guide their dog back to the source. That's microcurrents in action.

Temperature Layers: The Scent Sandwich

In big indoor spaces – like gyms, stairwells, or even your living room – air doesn't mix evenly. Warm air rises. Cool air sinks. And scent? It settles into **invisible layers**, like a floating sandwich.

Your dog might sniff low in a chilly corner, then suddenly switch to air sniffing when they hit a warm patch nearer the ceiling. They're not being random – they're reading the temperature layers. It's like climbing a scent staircase, where each step holds a different layer of air and scent.

This layering effect is perfect for multi-level mysteries. Imagine a trail that starts in the basement, floats up through a vent, and lands on a curtain rod in the lounge. Your dog might alert in the middle of the room – but the real clue is above their head. That's when you, the recruit, must think like a scent scientist and guide your dog in 3D.

Pressure Zones: The Doorway Pause

Ever noticed your dog pause dramatically at a doorway? That's not just dramatic flair – it's **science**. Doorways often act like scent bottlenecks. When a door opens, it creates a pressure change that pulls scent into or out of a room. It's like opening a **vacuum tube** for smells.

Dogs can sense this shift instantly. They'll pause, sniff, and decide whether the trail continues or disappears. As a recruit, your job is to watch for these moments. If your dog hesitates at a threshold, don't rush them. They're calculating the drift.

One of our senior Sniff Squaders, Agent Dexter, once left a cookie crumb near a heater in the lounge. But when the door opened, the scent whooshed into the hallway. The recruit's dog searched the wrong room at first — but then cracked the case by tracing the airflow. That's pressure zone magic.

Dead Zones: The Quiet Corners

Not all rooms are created equal. Some corners, closets, or behind-the-couch zones have almost no airflow. These are called scent dead zones. Scent can get trapped there – or never reach them at all.

Dogs often ignore these spots unless encouraged. That's where your leadership comes in. If the trail seems to vanish, check the **dead zones**. You might find a hidden clue waiting in the still air.

In one mission, Agent Dexter hid a treat behind a curtain in a corner with no airflow. The dog missed it – until the recruit gently guided them back. One sniff later, mystery solved.

Phantom Clues: Scent from Above (or Below)

Here's a twist: scent doesn't just move sideways. It travels up and down. Through vents, stairwells, and even floorboards, scent can drift **vertically**, creating phantom clues.

Your dog might first notice the scent in the kitchen, but the source is actually in the attic. Or they might sniff near a vent, catching a whiff from the basement. That's when you need to think in 3D. Where could the scent be coming from? What's above you? What's below?

This kind of mystery is perfect for experienced recruits. It teaches you to trust your dog's nose, but also to use your brain. It seems the Crumb Bandit loves vertical tricks – but you're onto him now.

SUPER SNIFFER SCIENCE ALERT!

Did you know:
The noses of professional sniffer dogs can sniff out weird things like USBs buried in eskies full of food, cash stashed inside staircases and SIM cards inside shoe soles. All these items release scent molecules that the dog can be trained to smell! **FACT!**

Scent Detective Secrets

Real-life scent detection dogs – like police K9s, search-and-rescue teams, and conservation dogs – use **air currents** to their advantage every day. In indoor searches, handlers often open windows or doors to stir up scent and help dogs catch the trail. They watch how the dog moves through the space, noting when the nose goes up (air sniffing) or down (ground sniffing), and adjust their search strategy based on airflow.

In crime scenes, investigators sometimes use smoke sticks or powder trails to visualize how air moves through a room. This helps them understand where scent might have travelled – and where it might be hiding. You won't need smoke sticks for your mission, but you *will* need sharp eyes, a curious mind, and a dog with a nose that's ready to roll. Even elite search dogs know that scent can pool in corners, drift under doors, or float up to ceiling fans. That's why they often pause, circle, or sniff the air before diving into action. They're not confused – they're calculating the mystery!

Super Sniffer Mystery
The Drift Zone Heist

Incoming Mystery Alert!:

Dr Whiff has just picked up a suspicious scent swirl in the lounge. After last night's banana-on-the-ceiling-fan stunt and crumb scatter under the curtain, the Crumb Bandit is back - and this time, the clues are drifting. A faint whiff of peanut butter on toast was detected... but the source? Unknown.

Sniff Squad Orders:

Track the scent trail through tricky indoor air currents. Your mission is to decode how smells move, pool, vanish, and float - then guide your dog to the final clue. You'll need sharp eyes, steady leadership, and a nose that's ready to roll.

Mission Kit Checklist:

- ☐ A quiet indoor space with 3 hiding spots: one open, one tucked in a corner, one above or below normal nose level
- ☐ Two scent items that are the same (e.g. 2 pieces of peanut butter on toast) – one to use as the scent article and the other to hide
- ☐ A fan, heater, or open door to stir the air
- ☐ Your field journal to record sniffing styles & success

Parent Tips for Younger Recruits:

If your child is allergic to peanuts, try a smelly sock, a dog-safe treat in a paper towel or some other strong scent on a cotton ball.

Sniff Instructions:

1. Pick a quiet indoor area with no distractions and three good hiding spots—one open, one tucked into a corner, and one above or below nose level.
2. Hide the scent target in the first location and let it sit for 5–10 minutes so the scent can settle or drift.
3. Bring your dog into the room, let them sniff the scent article, cue the search and observe how they move.
4. If your dog gets stuck or misses a zone, gently encourage but let them lead the search.
5. Repeat the search for Levels 2 and 3, changing the hiding spot and adjusting airflow - open a door, turn on a fan, or switch off a heater.
6. When your dog locates the scent, reward them with praise, play, or treats.
7. Write down what you noticed in your field journal—where the scent was hidden, how your dog searched, and what surprised you.

Level 1

The Scent Pool

- Hide the scent item behind a curtain or under a low table.
- Keep the room quiet - no fans or open doors.
- Watch for your dog pausing or circling where scent has pooled.

Level 2

The Dead Zone

- Tuck the scent into a closet corner or behind furniture.
- Encourage your dog to check areas they might normally skip.
- Notice if they need help spotting clues in still-air zones.

Level 3

Vertical Drift

- Place the scent on a shelf, stair, or near a vent.
- Use a fan or heater to stir the air and create drift.
- Watch for your dog alerting in one spot - but the clue is above or below.

Badge Readiness Checklist

Great work, Recruit! You cracked the case, tracked the drift, and guided your dog like a true scent scientist. Before you earn your **Air Current Cadet** badge, let's make sure you've mastered the key skills from this mission. Ready for your Drift Zone checklist? Let's go!

I'm ready!

- ❏ I spotted a scent pool and watched how my dog responded.
- ❏ I searched a dead zone and guided my dog into quiet corners.
- ❏ I tracked a vertical drift—above or below normal nose level.
- ❏ I noticed how doors, fans, or heaters changed the scent trail.
- ❏ I let my dog lead the search and watched their sniff signals.
- ❏ I adjusted my strategy when the scent seemed to vanish.
- ❏ I recorded my observations in my Field Journal like a true scent scientist.

Badge Unlocked: Air Current Cadet!

Congratulations, Recruit! You've officially earned your **Air Current Cadet** badge—proof that you've mastered the invisible forces that shape every indoor scent trail. You now understand how microcurrents, scent pools, dead zones, and vertical drift can hide or reveal clues. That means you're not just following your dog—you're thinking like a scent scientist, guiding with strategy, and solving mysteries in 3D.

Mission Debrief: Operation Airwave Complete!

You did it, Recruit! You and your dog just sniffed your way through one of the trickiest chapters yet – **indoor scent detection**. This wasn't just about chasing runaway cheese or locating a banana on a ceiling fan. You cracked the science of how scent behaves indoors, where smells don't stay put – they swirl through microcurrents, sneak behind curtains, pool in quiet corners, and float up walls like invisible clues.

You've officially earned your **Air Current Cadet** badge, and with it, the kind of scent detection skills you'll need to **catch and unmask the Crumb Bandit**. You learned to read your dog's sniff signals – nose up for air sniffing, nose down for ground clues – and adjust your strategy when the trail goes cold. You discovered how temperature layers create scent sandwiches, how doorways act like scent vacuums, and how dead zones can hide clues in plain sight.

And guess what? The Crumb Bandit is getting nervous. He thought indoor tricks would throw you off. But you stayed sharp, curious, and calm – and you foiled his snack sabotage once again.

But something's changed. The Bandit's moves are getting bolder, sneakier, and more playful. Was this a test? A warning? A challenge? One thing's for sure – he's not done yet. And neither are you.

You're closing in. With every mission, you're building the skills, confidence, and teamwork it takes to outsmart him. So grab your gear, steady your dog, and get ready. The next mystery is coming – and it's going to take everything you've learned to stay one sniff ahead!

Chapter Eight

Grid Sweep Ops
Learn the Pro-Level Search Styles That Leave No Clue Behind

Welcome back, Recruit! You've cracked one of the toughest scent puzzles – tracking how smells swirl and drift indoors. From microcurrents to vertical clues, you proved you can sniff like a scent scientist and lead like a legend. Now it's time to level up again. Real scent detectives don't wander – they grid. In this chapter, you'll learn three smart search patterns that turn any room into a mystery zone. Ready to sweep, spiral, and zone in? Let's grid and go!

Mission #7: Operation Grid Sweep

Incoming Mission, Recruit! Dr. Whiff just sent word from HQ — a new Mystery Alert is about to drop. The Crumb Bandit was spotted near the snack cabinet in Sector 7, leaving behind a swirl of cinnamon scent and a half-eaten cracker. Agent Dexter nearly nabbed him, but he slipped into a maze of furniture and airflow. He's still in there... He's getting bolder.

Your mission is to launch **Operation Grid Sweep.** Before the next Mystery Alert hits, you'll learn three pro search patterns — Square Grid, Spiral, and Zone — to cover every inch of indoor terrain. No cushion, curtain, or corner goes unchecked.

The Bandit's scent tricks are evolving: dead zones, vertical drift, cluttered layouts. But with your new skills, you'll track his moves, read your dog's signals, and log every clue like a seasoned scent detective.

The chase is on. Let's flush him out!

Indoor Search Grid Techniques

Now that you understand how scent moves indoors, it's time to learn how to search smart. Professional scent detectives don't just wander around a room hoping to stumble onto clues – they use **search grids** to make sure every inch of the room gets sniffed. And today, you'll learn how to guide your dog through three different **search patterns** that turn your home into a mystery-solving zone.

Square Grid Search

In small, open rooms like bedrooms or living spaces, the **Square Grid Search** is your go-to strategy. Picture the floor as a giant checkerboard. You and your dog will move methodically from one square to the next, starting in a corner and sweeping across the room in straight lines. Every few steps, pause and give your dog time to sniff the air and the ground – this isn't a race, it's a mission. Some recruits like to mark each square with sticky notes or tape to track their progress, which adds a fun, visual layer to the search. This method ensures no scent pool is left behind, especially in corners where clues love to hide. As always, let your dog take the lead. If they pause or start sniffing deeply, hold back and give them space to investigate. That moment of focus might be the breakthrough you've been waiting for.

Spiral Search

When you're working in larger, open areas like hallways or spacious living rooms, it's time to **spiral** in. Begin at the center of the room and slowly circle outward, expanding your search like a snail shell. As you move, your dog will have the chance to catch scent that's pooled in the middle or drifted toward the edges. Encourage them to check under cushions, around furniture legs, and along the baseboards – scent has a sneaky way of settling in unexpected places. Keep an eye on your dog's **sniffing style.** If their nose shifts from high in the air to low on the ground, they're likely closing in on something important. That switch is your signal to slow down and let them work the trail.

Zone Search

For multi-room missions or cluttered spaces filled with furniture, toys, or obstacles, the **Zone Search** is your best strategy. Break the area into smaller sections – maybe a couch zone, a bookshelf zone, or a table zone – and search one at a time. After each zone is cleared, mark it in your field journal and move on to the next. This approach keeps your mission **organized** and helps you notice **patterns** in your dog's behavior.

Maybe they always pause near vents or circle around doorways – those are clues worth tracking. And if your dog gets stuck or distracted, don't worry. Take a short break, reset the energy, and restart the mission with a fresh cue like, "Sniff Squad – activate!"

SUPER SNIFFER SCIENCE ALERT!

Did you know: In indoor missions, trained scent dogs use structured search patterns to ensure no corner goes unsniffed. Their handlers guide them through rooms with grid searches, zone sweeps and spiral patterns – just like you're mastering now! **FACT!**

Search Style Decoder

As you guide your dog through each search style, pay close attention to their **sniff signals**. Fast sniffing usually means they're scanning for scent, while slow, deep sniffing suggests they've found something worth investigating. If they start circling or pause in one spot, they're likely zeroing in on the source. A tail wag or curious head tilt might be their way of saying, "I'm onto something!" Keep your field journal handy and jot down what you observe. Did they sniff high near the curtains? Pause near the heater? These details help you understand how scent moves indoors – and how your dog is learning to solve the mystery, one sniff at a time.

Super Sniffer Mystery
Search Style Showdown

Incoming Mystery Alert!:

Attention! The Crumb Bandit was last seen darting through Sector 7—the snack zone near the living room. Agents recovered a cinnamon-scented tissue tucked behind a couch cushion. The scent trail was faint but fresh. This was a close encounter and the Bandit is believed to still be in there!

Sniff Squad Orders:

Deploy Operation Grid Sweep immediately. Use all three search styles—Square Grid, Spiral, and Zone Search—to flush the Bandit out of his hiding spot.

Mission Kit Checklist:

- ☐ Cinnamon-scented cotton buds x 2 (scent article and target)
- ☐ Sticky notes, cones or tape to mark search zones
- ☐ Leash to keep your dog close and guide them carefully through each of the search patterns
- ☐ Clear cue to start the mission ("Sniff Squad activate!" or "Search!")
- ☐ Your field journal to record sniffing styles & success

Parent Tips for Younger Recruits:

Help your child dip their cotton buds into some ground cinnamon or essential oil and wrap them in a tissue. Store in plastic ziplock bags until needed. They may also require help marking out the search patterns.

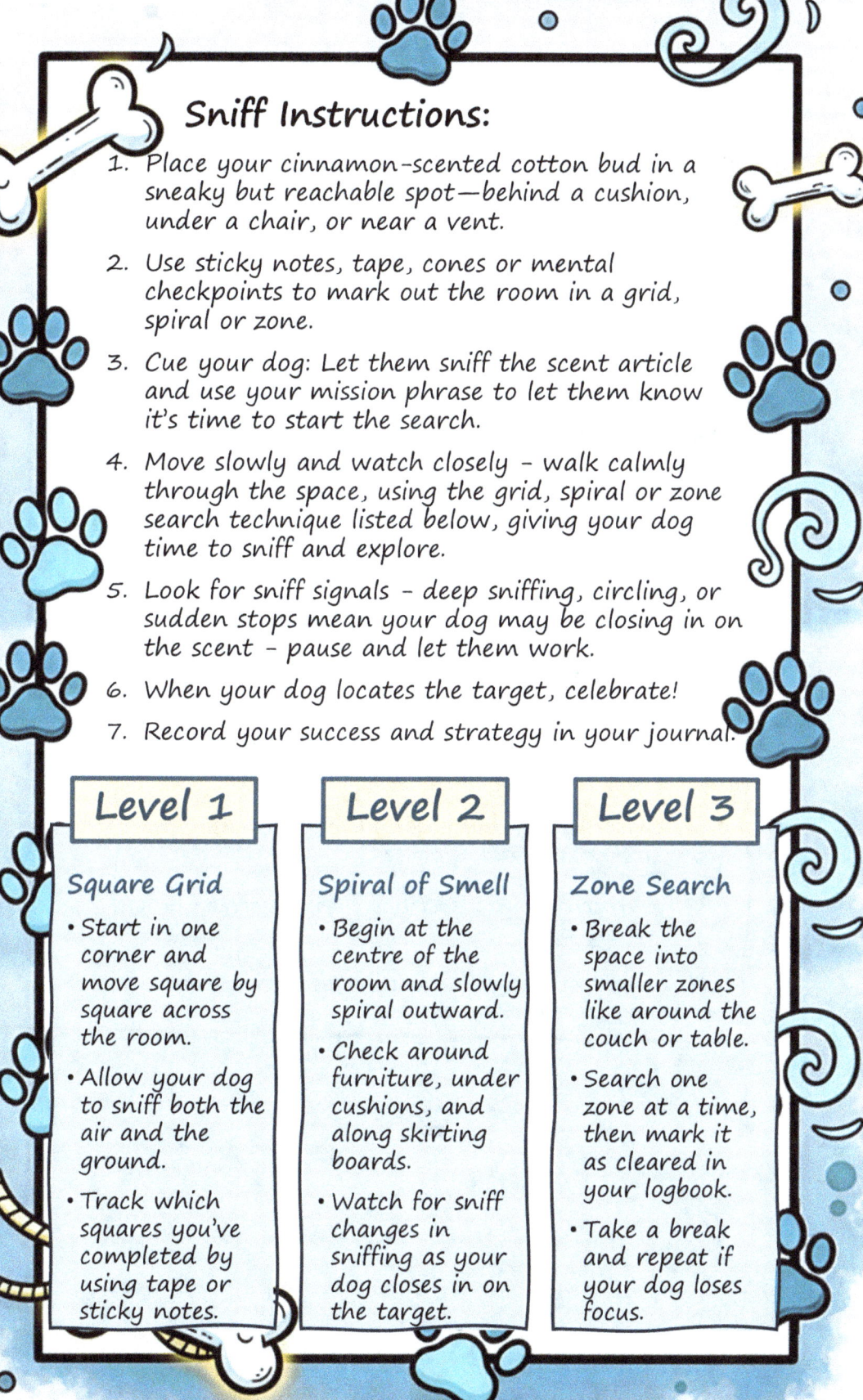

Badge Readiness Checklist

Congratulations, Recruit! You've completed *Operation Grid Sweep* and mastered all three search styles. You tracked scent like a pro, logged your clues, and closed in on the Crumb Bandit. Now it's time to earn your **Grid Sweep Specialist** badge—check off each task to make it official!

I'm ready!

- ❏ I used a confident, clear mission cue to start the search (like "Search!").
- ❏ I guided my dog through a full Square Grid search, covering each section step by step.
- ❏ I completed a Spiral Search, starting in the centre and circling outward.
- ❏ I broke a space into zones and searched each one carefully, marking them as cleared.
- ❏ I watched for sniff signals like deep sniffing, circling, or sudden pauses.
- ❏ I wrote down at least one clue or pattern in my logbook.
- ❏ I celebrated the find with praise, treats, or play to reinforce success.

Badge Unlocked: Grid Sweep Specialist!

You did it, Recruit! You've officially earned your **Grid Sweep Specialist** badge. That means you know how to search smart—using Square, Spiral, and Zone techniques to cover every inch of a space.

Mission Debrief: Operation Grid Sweep Complete!

Outstanding work, Recruit! You've completed one of the most strategic missions in the Sniff Squad training schedule – and HQ couldn't be prouder. This wasn't just about sniffing. It was about thinking like a scent detective, guiding your dog with purpose, and mastering the art of indoor search.

You learned how to break down complex spaces using **Square Grid**, **Spiral**, and **Zone** search patterns – each one designed to help you cover every inch of terrain with precision. You practiced reading sniff signals, logging clues, and adjusting your strategy in real time. You didn't just search – you led.

That's why you've earned the **Grid Sweep Specialist** badge. It marks a major step forward in your training. You now have the skills to track scent in layered environments, decode your dog's behavior, and flush out even the sneakiest targets.

During the final sweep of Sector 7, there was a moment – a creak of the door, a rush of air – and then a flicker of purple. The Crumb Bandit escaped. Unfortunate, yes. But you saw him. You were close. Closer than ever.

And now, the chase intensifies. The Crumb Bandit is running out of places to hide.

Next up: **Operation Weather Watch**. You'll learn how scent behaves in wind, rain, and snow – and how to adapt your search strategy like a true field agent. Expect puddles, gusts, and maybe even a snowstorm. It's messy, it's scientific, and it's going to be fun.

Badge unlocked. Mission complete. Stay sharp, Recruit. The final showdown is near.

CHAPTER NINE

It's All Elementary
Wind, Weather and the Art of Deduction

THE GAME IS AFOOT, Recruit! You've cracked clues, swept grids, and chased scent trails through HQ. You've guided your dog with precision and outsmarted distractions like a true Sniff Squad Detective. But now the trail has shifted. The Crumb Bandit has vanished indoors — and fresh evidence points outside. Out here, **weather** becomes part of the mystery. **Wind, temperature, and terrain** shape how scent moves and disappears. To catch the Bandit, you'll need to read the skies, feel the breeze, and adapt your strategy on the fly. This is where scentwork gets real — and your training goes from skilled… to legendary.

Mission #8: Operation Weather Watch

Heads up Recruit! The trail has gone cold indoors. After a string of near-captures, the Crumb Bandit has vanished from HQ's corridors, snack stations, and training zones. But just when it seemed like he'd slipped through our paws for good… new evidence has just surfaced.

Early this morning, a half-eaten biscuit was discovered near Trail Sector 4. A swirl of scent lingered in the grass. And caught on the fence? A single thread of purple fabric – fluttering in the breeze like a taunt. Dr. Whiff has confirmed it - the Crumb Bandit has moved **outdoors**.

That means it's time for **Operation Weather Watch** – your first real outdoor mission. From this point forward, the **environment** becomes part of the mystery. Wind, temperature, rain, and terrain all shape how scent travels, settles, and disappears. If you want to lead your dog like a true Sniff Squad Detective, you'll need to learn how to read the sky, feel the air, and adjust your strategy in real time.

In this chapter, you'll discover how a gentle breeze can carry scent in long, sniffable waves – and how strong gusts can scatter it in every direction. You'll learn how still air causes scent to pool in low spots like grass, bushes, or under rocks, and how your dog instinctively switches from air sniffing to ground tracking when the trail drops. You'll explore how **temperature** plays tricks on scent: why cool days are perfect for sniffing, how heat makes scent rise and fade, and how cold snaps can trap scent beneath frost or dew. You'll even learn how rain can help or hinder a search – pushing scent into the ground for easier tracking, or washing it away entirely.

This mission will sharpen your ability to read your dog's body language in the elements – watching for nose lifts, tail flicks, zigzags, and sudden pauses that signal scent detection. You'll practice adjusting your pace, choosing smart starting points, and using natural features like fences, trees, and windbreaks to your advantage.

Why does this matter? Because the Crumb Bandit is no longer hiding in plain sight. He's using the elements to his advantage. But with these new skills, you'll be able to follow his trail through wind, heat, and rain – and close in on him faster than ever before.

We're getting close, Recruit. Very close. So grab your gear, check the weather and get ready to sniff smart. The chase is back on – and you are getting close to having learnt everything you need to capture the Bandit.

Weather Watch: How Weather Shapes the Chase

When you head outside for a scent mission, the weather becomes part of the mystery. Wind, heat, rain – even snow and terrain – can twist, stretch, or hide scent in ways that challenge even the sharpest sniffer. If you want to guide your dog like a true Sniff Squad Detective, you'll need to learn how to read the sky, feel the ground, and sniff smart in every condition. Let's break it down.

Wind: The Invisible Clue Mover

Wind is sneaky. You can't see it, but it's constantly shaping the scent trail. On breezy days, scent travels in smooth, sniffable waves – like invisible rivers flowing through the air. Dogs love this! Their noses go up, tails wag, and they can catch a whiff from far away. But when the wind gets wild, it scatters scent like confetti. Your dog might zigzag, circle, or pause to figure out where the trail went.

If the wind is strong, try starting your search **downwind** – so the scent blows toward your dog. Watch how your dog reacts: nose up means they're catching airborne clues; nose down means the scent has settled. And on still days, when the air isn't moving, scent pools in low spots like grass, bushes, or under rocks. That's when your dog becomes a ground-sniffing explorer, nose to the earth, tracking like a pro.

Temperature: The Scent Shifter

Temperature is a trickster. On cool days – around 18°C or 65°F – your dog is in their sniffing sweet spot. **Scent molecules** stay active, and your dog's nose works at full power. But when the sun blazes and the air gets dry, scent rises and fades fast. Your dog might sniff higher or move quickly, trying to catch the trail before it vanishes into the heat.

If it's hot, look for shaded areas or cooler surfaces like grass or mulch – places where scent might still be hiding. On cold days, scent doesn't travel far and can get trapped under frost or dew. But don't worry – your dog's nose is still amazing. They'll sniff close to the ground, paw at the surface, and even use body heat to melt frozen clues. If it's chilly, give your dog time to investigate slowly. The trail might be faint, but it's still there.

Rain: The Scent Soaker

Rain changes everything. After a shower, scent gets pushed into the ground, making it easier to track on soil, grass, or leaves. Dogs often sniff low and move with confidence, like they're reading a soggy scent map. But puddles and wet surfaces can wash scent away, especially on concrete or smooth paths.

If it's just rained, start your search in grassy or leafy areas where scent sticks better. Watch for your dog's nose to stay low and steady. But if the rain is heavy or fresh puddles are everywhere, be ready for detours. Your dog might skip ahead or circle back to find a stronger clue. Stay flexible – and trust their instincts.

Snow: The Frozen Puzzle

Snowy missions are slower but magical. Scent hides under the surface, like buried **treasure** waiting to be found. Dogs will sniff, dig, and investigate like true detectives. You might see them pause near tree trunks or bushes, where scent pools form in warmer spots. Cold air makes scent cling to surfaces, so your dog may sniff low and use their paws to uncover hidden trails.

If you're searching in snow, let your dog take the lead. They'll know where to dig and where to pause. Look for places where the snow is thinner or where sunlight hits – those spots often hold stronger scent clues. And remember, patience is key. Snow slows things down, but it also makes every discovery feel epic.

Terrain: The Ground Beneath the Mystery

Terrain is the secret partner in every search. Grass holds scent like a **sponge**, while concrete lets it slip away fast. Leaves, mulch, and dirt are great scent holders – especially after rain. Bushes and fences can trap scent in corners, and tree trunks act like **scent magnets**. Your dog will use the landscape like a map, sniffing high and low depending on where the scent sticks.

In movies, you may have seen villains escape by crossing rivers, leaving tracking dogs stuck — but that's only partly true. Fast-moving water can wash away scent, but trained dogs can still catch airborne particles or pick up scent on the far bank. Rivers make tracking tricky, not impossible.

SNIFF SQUAD: DOG TRAINING FOR KIDS WHO LOVE MYSTERIES 103

As a handler, your job is to notice where scent might hide. If your dog pauses near a fence post or sniffs around a bush, don't rush them. They're reading the terrain, checking for **scent pools**, and following the trail with precision. The more you understand the ground beneath your paws, the better you'll guide your dog through the mystery.

SUPER SNIFFER SCIENCE ALERT!

Did you know:
After sunrise, warming ground releases trapped scent molecules into the air—creating a brief "scent bloom." Early morning searches can reveal clues that were hidden overnight.
Timing is everything! **FACT!**

Your Role: Weather-Wise Detective

No matter the weather, your dog knows what to do. They'll switch between air sniffing when scent floats, ground sniffing when it settles, and circling when they're closing in. Your job is to watch, learn, and guide with care. Before your next outdoor mission, take a moment to check the sky. Is it breezy or still? Warm or cool? Damp or dry? These clues will help you plan your search and understand your dog's sniffing superpowers.

Super Sniffer Mystery
Gone With The Wind

Incoming Mystery Alert!:

The Crumb Bandit has escaped HQ and slipped into the backyard! A half-eaten biscuit lies near the fence, and a thread from his purple cape is caught in the wire. The scent trail is fresh—but the wind is shifting. He's out there, hiding in the garden's shadows. Time to gear up and sniff him out! We're finally getting close to catching him!

Sniff Squad Orders:

Begin your scent search at the fenceline. Guide your dog toward the garden shed or far corner of the yard, using scent clues, wind direction, and terrain to track the hidden target.

Mission Kit Checklist:

- ☐ Your scent item (a biscuit crumb or scent cloth)
- ☐ A leash or harness for controlled tracking
- ☐ Weather-appropriate gear (hat, water, towel)
- ☐ Cones, flags, or markers for the search zone
- ☐ Treats and praise for sniffing rewards
- ☐ Your field journal to record sniffing styles & success notes

Parent Tips for Younger Recruits:

Help your child choose a starting point that is downwind from your garden shed or yard corner, with easy access to the hiding spot.

Sniff Instructions:

1. Stand near the fence in your backyard with your biscuit crumb or scent cloth (scent article).
2. Drag or walk the scent article toward your garden shed or yard corner, rubbing it on plants, tree trunks, garden beds or outdoor furniture on the way to leave a scent trail.
3. For levels 2 and 3 below, mark scent-rich spots like mulch, grass, under bushes or near warm surfaces, with cones or flags, and ensure you rub scent from your scent article into those spots.
4. Hide your scent article in the yard corner or shed.
5. Cue your dog and let them explore, guiding gently and watching for sniffing style changes.
6. Note where they pause or shift - those are hot zones - and record details in your field journal.
7. When they find the scent article, reward your partner and celebrate like a hero team!

Level 1

Breeze Breaker

- Start at the fence and guide your dog gently toward the shed/corner.
- Let scent from the scent article drift downwind toward you.
- Watch for nose-up sniffing and zigzag moves as your dog picks up the scent.

Level 2

Terrain Tracker

- Drag scent over mulch, rocks, and tree trunks from the fence to the shed/corner.
- Press scent at each terrain change to create a scent zone.
- Guide your dog through each scent zone and note how many they find.

Level 3

Weather Wizard

- Set trail in wind, drizzle or cool air
- Use terrain to help scent stick when laying your trail.
- Watch how your dog adapts and allow them to lead the way.
- Gently guide until they find the scent article.

Badge Readiness Checklist

Nice work, Recruit! But before you earn your **Weather Scout** badge, you'll need to prove you can sniff smart in the outdoors. That means reading the wind, adjusting for temperature, and guiding your dog through tricky terrain like mulch, rocks, and shifting surfaces. This checklist will help you prep for real-world scentwork – where every breeze, puddle, and patch of grass could hold a clue.

I'm ready!

- ☐ I can identify how wind affects scent and adjust the search direction to match.
- ☐ I understand how temperature changes impact scent movement and pooling.
- ☐ I know how rain affects scent trails and where scent is likely to collect.
- ☐ I can guide my dog through snow or cold terrain while spotting scent-holding surfaces.
- ☐ I recognize terrain features—like mulch, rocks, and bushes—that trap or carry scent.
- ☐ I can spot when my dog switches sniffing styles and know what each one means.
- ☐ I can set up a scent trail using wind, terrain, and weather to challenge my dog's nose.

Badge Unlocked: Weather Scout!

Well done, Recruit! You've mastered outdoor scent detection – navigating wind, terrain, and tricky hide-outs like a true Sniff Squad Detective. You've been awarded the **Weather Scout** badge. Get ready – your next adventure is just ahead!

Mission Debrief: Operation Weather Watch Complete!

Great work, Recruit! You've just wrapped up your outdoor detection training – and what an adventure it's been. From swirling breezes to soggy bushes, you've transformed your backyard into a dynamic **scent playground**. You've seen first-hand how wind, temperature, and natural obstacles can twist the trail, shape the search, and sharpen your dog's super-sniffing skills.

Throughout this mission, you learned that creating challenging hides isn't about making things impossible – it's about **building confidence** through success. Starting simple and celebrating every win has helped your team grow stronger with each search. Some days were breezy (literally), and others felt like solving a puzzle in motion. But every twist in the trail was a chance to learn, adapt, and deepen the bond between you and your dog.

You uncovered how scent pools form in shady spots, how bark and bushes can trap clues, and how weather can send scent drifting in unexpected directions. You practiced reading your dog's **body language** – watching for the nose dip, the tail twitch, the pause that says "I'm onto something." You guided them through terrain, set up safe and smart search zones, and used trees, fences, and garden features to create thrilling challenges. These weren't just backyard games – they were the building blocks of real-world detection work.

And guess what? You cracked another case! But don't get too comfortable. We can't rest on our laurels – yet. Each training session is sharpening the skills we'll need to finally catch this snack-snatching villain. We're getting closer. The clues are adding up. The trail is now red hot! What will the Crumb Bandit do next? Is he playing a game… or setting a trap?

You've come a long way, Recruit. From basic indoor searches to full-blown outdoor missions, you've proven that you're not just playing – you're training. You're not just hiding treats – you're building a partnership. And you're not just following a trail – you're becoming a real detective.

As you prepare for the final training session, keep sniffing, keep celebrating, and keep leading your team with heart. The trail ahead is full of mysteries – and the Crumb Bandit's days of freedom are numbered.

And don't forget the importance of wind, weather and terrain. In the words of the world's most famous Detective, Sherlock Holmes, "*It's all elementary*"!

CHAPTER TEN

Operation Crumb Bandit
The Final Trail... or Is It?

THIS IS IT, RECRUIT. **The mission that changes everything!** You've sniffed through shadows, zigzagged across backyards, cracked puzzles, and earned your stripes. From curious beginner to confident scent detective, you've trained for this moment. This is your **Final Mission** – one last trail, one last mystery, one final chance to prove you're ready to join the elite rank of certified **Sniff Squad Detective**. And the target? The snack-snatching trickster who's dodged every trap since your first mission: the infamous **Crumb Bandit**. The chase ends here! Will you successfully track down the Bandit?

Mission #10: Operation Crumb Bandit

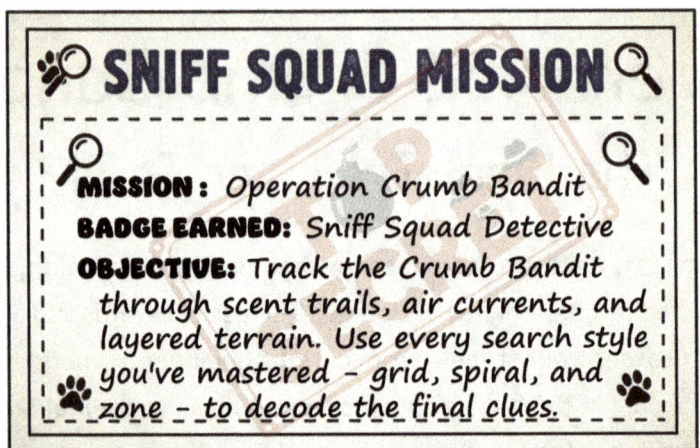

Recruit, from the very first day at Sniff Squad HQ, you've been preparing for this moment. You learned how scent travels—how it floats on air currents, pools in shady corners, and clings to terrain like a secret. You mastered grid, spiral and zone searches. You trained your dog to sniff through chaos, indoors and outdoors, and lock onto scent articles. You decoded the canine brain, learned what motivates your dog the most, and read every sniff, pause, and tail wag like a clue in a mystery novel.

Meanwhile, the Crumb Bandit has been busy. He's scattered muffin and cookie crumbs in the training yard, planted banana peels on ceiling fans, and left chaos in his wake. He's used decoys, distractions, and snack sabotage to stay one sniff ahead. No recruit has caught him. Not yet. **Until now.**

But heads up Recruit! A high-priority alert just came through from Dr. Whiff at HQ!

Hidden beneath a pile of mulch in the garden, **Agent Dexter** recovered a half-nibbled stinky sock inside an empty cheese packet. That's right – we have ourselves a verified scent article! It's pungent, unmistakable, and packed with clues. For the first time ever, we have a direct trail to the Crumb Bandit. And you're the one who's going to follow it.

This final mission will test everything you've learned. You'll need to present the scent article to your canine offsider with confidence, read the terrain like a map of mysteries, decode clues hidden in everyday objects, and guide your dog to the Bandit's lair. The Bandit knows we're close. He's pulled out every trick in the **treat pouch** – false leads, rogue scents, and snack-scented chaos. But you? You've trained for this. You've built the skills, the focus, and the teamwork to see through the mess.

This is it, Recruit. The final trail. The ultimate test. The Crumb Bandit's days of freedom are numbered! So zip up your treat pouch. Cue your mission phrase. Grab that sock and stuff some cheese into it. The chase is real. The mystery is alive. And the final trail starts now!

Sniffing in 3D: Natural Obstacles and Vertical Trails

Recruit, before we set you and your canine partner after the Crumb Bandit, there's one more thing you'll need to learn if you want to capture him – natural obstacles and vertical trails. Welcome back to one of the most exciting training zones in the Sniff Squad universe: your own backyard. Out here, nature isn't just scenery – it's part of the mission. Trees, bushes, benches, fences, flowerpots… they're all **secret agents** in disguise, helping you and your dog become smarter, faster, and more adaptable sniffers.

Let's start with trees. They're not just tall – they're scent towers. Scent can climb the bark, swirl around branches, or settle in the shade at the base.

Your dog might sniff low, then suddenly stretch upward, nose twitching, tail wagging. That's your signal: the scent is **vertical**. Try hiding a scent article behind the trunk, in a knot, or on a low branch. Watch your dog read the bark like a mystery novel, decoding every groove and crack. After rain, bark holds scent even better – like a sponge full of clues.

Then there are bushes. Leafy, twisty, full of hiding spots. Scent gets trapped in the shade, caught on leaves, and tucked into mulch. When your dog dives nose-first into a bush, they're not just being dramatic – they're investigating a leafy labyrinth. You might see them circle, sniff, pause, then plunge deeper. Let them explore. Bushes teach patience and precision. They're perfect for warm days when scent rises elsewhere but stays cool and strong in the shade.

And don't forget the yard features you walk past every day. Benches become elevated hiding spots. Flowerpots hold scent in their soil. Fences bounce scent sideways, creating zigzag trails. Even the garden hose can twist the scent path like a sneaky snake. Try placing a scent article behind a bench leg, inside a flowerpot, or along the base of a fence. Your dog will sniff the air, then drop low or stretch high depending on where the scent is strongest. These features teach your dog to switch sniffing styles – just like real-world scent detectives.

Out here, every object becomes a clue. Every breeze becomes a hint. And every sniff becomes a step closer to solving the mystery. You're learning to read your dog's signals – nose lifts, tail wags, sudden pauses – and guide them through the mission with confidence. Your dog is learning to sniff in shade, sun, wind, and weird angles. Together, you're becoming a team that sees the invisible and sniffs the impossible.

So grab your field journal, it's time Recruit! The trail is tangled. The clues are clever. And the final mission is yours to solve! It's time to catch and unmask the Bandit!

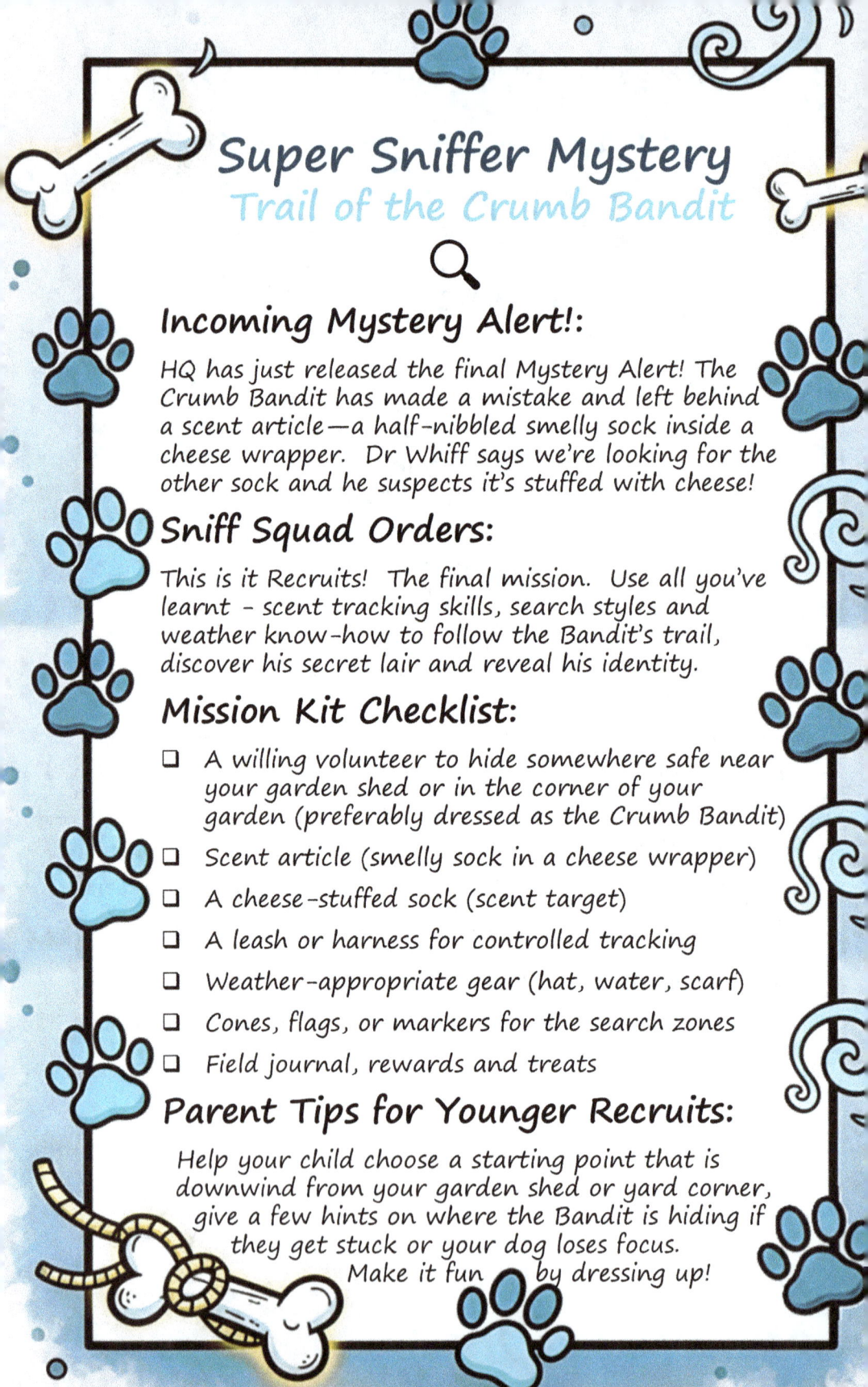

Super Sniffer Mystery
Trail of the Crumb Bandit

Incoming Mystery Alert!:

HQ has just released the final Mystery Alert! The Crumb Bandit has made a mistake and left behind a scent article—a half-nibbled smelly sock inside a cheese wrapper. Dr Whiff says we're looking for the other sock and he suspects it's stuffed with cheese!

Sniff Squad Orders:

This is it Recruits! The final mission. Use all you've learnt - scent tracking skills, search styles and weather know-how to follow the Bandit's trail, discover his secret lair and reveal his identity.

Mission Kit Checklist:

- ☐ A willing volunteer to hide somewhere safe near your garden shed or in the corner of your garden (preferably dressed as the Crumb Bandit)
- ☐ Scent article (smelly sock in a cheese wrapper)
- ☐ A cheese-stuffed sock (scent target)
- ☐ A leash or harness for controlled tracking
- ☐ Weather-appropriate gear (hat, water, scarf)
- ☐ Cones, flags, or markers for the search zones
- ☐ Field journal, rewards and treats

Parent Tips for Younger Recruits:

Help your child choose a starting point that is downwind from your garden shed or yard corner, give a few hints on where the Bandit is hiding if they get stuck or your dog loses focus. Make it fun by dressing up!

Sniff Instructions:

1. Volunteer Crumb Bandit drags the scent target (smelly sock stuffed with cheese) from the starting point to where they are going to hide, rubbing the target on some elevated areas like tree trunks and bush branches and marking them with sticky notes, flags or cones.
2. Crumb Bandit hides when you're not looking.
3. Get ready at the starting point, let your dog sniff the scent article to lock onto it, and then confidently cue the search.
4. Praise your dog each time they find a marked scent pool as they lead you closer to the Bandit.
5. When they find the scent article and the Crumb Bandit, reward your canine partner!
6. Complete all three levels, creating new scent pools on each trail and having the Crumb Bandit hide in different spots each time.
7. Celebrate like there's no tomorrow! You've cracked the final mystery!!

Level 1

Sock & Seek

- Use a simple hiding spot—behind a bush, under a bench, or behind a tree.
- Look for sticky notes, flags, or cones marking scent pools.
- Use your dog's natural sniff style and praise every clue they find.

Level 2

Drift & Decoy

- Bandit hides in a trickier spot—upwind.
- Scent pools are placed higher up (branches, posts) to test your dog's air sniffing and vertical tracking skills.
- Watch for decoy crumbs or snack wrappers meant to distract.

Level 3

Secret Lair

- Crumb Bandit hides inside the shed or in the corner of the yard.
- Scent pools twist through multiple zones.
- Choose either a grid or zone search style to decode the trail and catch the Bandit.

Badge Readiness Checklist

Wow! You nailed it Recruit, and you've captured the Crumb Bandit!! Before you claim your final badge, however, it's time for one last check-in. Use this checklist to make sure you and your dog are truly ready for the responsibility of becoming a certified **Sniff Squad Detective**!

I'm a Sniff Squad Detective!

- ❑ I can explain how scent travels through air, terrain, and weather—and how it affects a search.
- ❑ I know how to present a scent article and cue my dog with confidence.
- ❑ I've practiced all three search styles: grid, spiral, and zone—and know when to use each one.
- ❑ I've tracked scent trails indoors and outdoors, including vertical and tricky terrain.
- ❑ I've learned how to spot scent pools, decode clues, and stay focused through distractions.
- ❑ I've built a strong partnership with my dog based on timing, trust, and tail-wagging teamwork.
- ❑ I've completed every mission, earned every badge, and chased the Crumb Bandit to his lair!

Badge Unlocked: Sniff Squad Detective!

Hooray! You tracked the Crumb Bandit through wind, terrain and vertical clues, and stayed focused through every twist and distraction. You worked as a true team – sniffing scents, trusting your dog, and never giving up. You achieved your mission and your training so far has been a triumph. You are now officially a certified **Sniff Squad Detective**.

Mission Debrief: Operation Crumb Bandit Complete!

Hold onto your treat pouch, Recruit – you did it! You tracked the Crumb Bandit through swirling winds, sneaky scent pools, and snack-scented chaos. You cracked clues, scaled terrain, and sniffed through every twist with grit and flair. You presented the scent article like a pro, trusted your dog's instincts, and followed the trail straight to the Bandit's lair. But you didn't just complete the mission… **You mastered it.**

From backyard zigzags to vertical searches, you and your dog became a scent-tracking dream team. You learned how smells drift, how weather shifts the trail, and how to guide with confidence. You built a bond powered by timing, trust, and tail-wagging teamwork. You earned badges, cracked cases, and became a certified **Sniff Squad Detective**.

And now, you've done what no recruit before you could – **You caught the Crumb Bandit.** The mystery has been solved… Or has it…?

Crumb Bandit Captured! The Final Showdown

How did it happen? You followed the clues with precision and determination – through shadows, vertical scent pools, and swirling air currents. Every trail brought you closer. And finally, you found him. Crumb-pawed. Cornered. His secret lair exposed.

You saw your canine partner freeze as you got closer to the Bandit's lair – nose twitching, tail high. You knew those were signs that the Bandit was near. You crept forward, heart pounding, half expecting the Bandit to pounce on you. But there he was, paws up, hiding with a half-eaten cheese sock, a blueberry muffin and a croissant. The Crumb Bandit. The snack thief. **The legend.**

You moved fast. One confident cue, one perfect treat toss, and your canine blocked the Bandit's escape route like a pro. In a flash, you apprehended the Crumb Bandit and tied him up with your trail rope. Then you logged the final clue and radioed HQ. **The Crumb Bandit was officially in custody.**

And Now, For The Great Unmasking...

So here you are, Detective. The moment the entire academy has been waiting for.

The courtyard is packed – trainers, recruits, badge-holders from every mission, even the janitor (still bitter about his banana muffin that vanished three missions ago). Everyone is buzzing. The scent trail has ended. The Bandit is caught. And now, it's time to reveal the **face behind the crumbs**.

You step forward. The Crumb Bandit wriggles in your trail rope, clutching the last stolen blueberry muffin. You reach for the mask. This is it. The snack thief who's outwitted the Squad since the first mission is finally going to be unmasked!

You tighten the rope. The Bandit squirms. The crowd leans in. Not a single tail wags. Not a single treat crunches.

And then... **POOF!**

A glittery explosion of snack dust fills the air. Blueberry muffin-scented smoke swirls around you. The Bandit twists, flips, and dives through a trapdoor hidden beneath the backyard pavers – vanishing in a blur of crumbs and chaos.

When the dust settles, all that remains is a trail of cheesy footprints and a sticky note scrawled in barbecue sauce:

"Nice try, Sniff Squad. Catch me if you can!"

Mission Update: The Chase Continues

Just when you thought the case was closed… disaster struck!

In a glittery cloud of snack dust and blueberry-scented smoke, the Crumb Bandit pulled off an escape that would make a magician jealous. One moment he was squirming in your trail rope, the next – gone. Vanished through a trapdoor, leaving behind only crumbs, chaos, and a sticky note taunting the entire Squad.

But that's not all he left with.

Somehow, in the swirl of smoke and snack debris, the Bandit snatched something no recruit was meant to see: the key to **The Vault**.

And this is not just any key. This one unlocks a top-secret device buried deep beneath HQ – a machine designed to decode encrypted scent signals and classified trail patterns. Rumour has it, it can even interpret **scent-masking** anomalies. And now, it's in the hands of a snack thief turned saboteur.

The Crumb Bandit isn't just stealing muffins anymore. He's after secrets. Systems. **Power**.

Unfortunately, you didn't get to unmask the Crumb Bandit. Not this time. But you did everything right. You tracked, trailed, and triumphed. You earned your final badge and proved you're more than a recruit – you're now a certified **Sniff Squad Detective**.

And the Bandit? He may have escaped, but he left behind something even more exciting than a trail: **A challenge.**

So zip up your treat pouch. Sharpen your sniff strategy. Keep your field journal close and your dog closer. Because somewhere out there, the Crumb Bandit is unlocking something big – and when he strikes again, you'll be ready.

The chase isn't over. It's just beginning.

Welcome to the next level. **Detective**!

Conclusion

YOU DID IT, DETECTIVE!

You've mastered the missions, cracked the toughest clues, and earned your place in the Sniff Squad. You and your dog are now part of an elite team – trained, trusted, and ready to track down trouble wherever it hides.

But this isn't the end. It's the beginning.

A new trail is stirring. The winds are shifting. And somewhere out there, the Crumb Bandit is planning his next move. When he strikes, we'll need your nose, your grit, and your canine partner.

Stay sharp. Stay curious. Stay on the scent.

Welcome to the Squad, Detective. The chase continues!

Agent Max

Chief Sniff Squad Commander

P.S. Detective – Heads Up!

Advanced training is about to begin, and it's unlike anything you've faced before. You'll be heading outdoors – parks, trails, unpredictable terrain – where scent behaves differently and distractions are everywhere. You'll learn how to lead searches in real-world conditions, decode scent drift, and – most importantly – track the most elusive target of all: humans.

But before you gear up, there's something you should know.

A new villain has just entered the scene. **Dr. Muzzle** – a former tracking dog turned rogue scent engineer. Once a top Sniff Squad tracker, he doesn't leave crumbs – he leaves chaos. His calling card? **The Muzzle Code**: cryptic scent puzzles and mismatched trails designed to scramble your instincts. And top secret intelligence just received by HQ indicates he's developed **human scent cloaking technology** – devices that make people undetectable to even the sharpest sniffer.

His goal? To make villains **invisible to noses**.

The Crumb Bandit may be on the run with the key to **The Vault**, but Dr. Muzzle is just getting started.

Get ready, Detective. The next Sniff Squad book will push your skills, test your focus, and unlock scent strategies you didn't know you had.

While one chase continues the other is heating up! See you very soon, **Detective!**

About the Author
Agent Max

Agent Max is an educator, writer, and lifelong mystery-lover who grew up founding backyard detective clubs and solving imaginary crimes with her trusty canine and notebook. Today, she channels that same spirit into creating playful, educational resources that help families learn and grow together. Inspired by her two very sniffy Beagliers – real-life scent detectives with a nose for fun – Agent Max blends mystery, problem-solving, and exploration into every page of Sniff Squad. Whether she's crafting badges, creating mystery characters, or testing scent games in the bush, she's passionate about helping kids bond with their dogs, build confidence, and discover the joy of learning through play.

Welcome to HQ
Unlock Your Recruit Rewards

Congratulations, Detective!

You've completed your training but your scentwork journey is just beginning!

Visit **Sniff Squad HQ** at

www.sniffsquad.com.au

your official headquarters for all things Sniff Squad.

- **Sniff Squad Merch:** Gear for adventures and missions – for you and your canine!

- **Sniff Squad Starter Packs:** Everything you need to undertake your Sniff Squad Academy training – badges, stickers, treat pouch, cap and more.

- **Sniff Squad Field Journal:** The perfect companion to this book, designed for logging clues, tracking progress, and unlocking bonus Sniff Squad mysteries and challenges.

- **Unlock Recruit Rewards:** Downloadable stickers, field journal pages, and bonus challenges await you online.

Scan the QR code to access your Sniff Squad Portal and collect rewards.

www.ingramcontent.com/pod-product-compliance
Lightning Source LLC
Chambersburg PA
CBHW071855070526
44583CB00016B/1707